Direct Selling

Direct Selling

A Global and Social Business Model

Sara L. Cochran
Anne T. Coughlan
Victoria L. Crittenden
William F. Crittenden
Linda K. Ferrell
O.C. Ferrell
W. Alan Luce
Robert A. Peterson

BEP

BUSINESS EXPERT PRESS

Leader in applied, concise business books

Direct Selling: A Global and Social Business Model

Copyright © Business Expert Press, LLC, 2022.

Cover photo by John A. Crittenden, 2021.

Cover design by Charlene Kronstedt

In geometry, a tessellation arranges tiles in a plane without any gaps according to a given set of rules. The tessellation is an appropriate depiction of direct selling companies as they are independent in terms of the variety of products offered but dependent in terms of their fit within the direct selling marketplace.

Interior design by Exeter Premedia Services Private Ltd., Chennai, India

First published in 2021 by
Business Expert Press, LLC
222 East 46th Street, New York, NY 10017
www.businessexpertpress.com

ISBN-13: 978-1-63742-113-0 (paperback)
ISBN-13: 978-1-63742-114-7 (e-book)

Business Expert Press Selling and Sales Force Management
Collection

Collection ISSN: 2161-8909 (print)
Collection ISSN: 2161-8917 (electronic)

First edition: 2021

10 9 8 7 6 5 4 3 2 1

Description

The Power of Direct Selling

Direct selling is not an *industry* per se nor is it merely a *go-to-market business model* and *channel* to reach consumers. It is bigger than any of this—direct selling is *people*. The ability for people with *entrepreneurial spirit* to build a successful business, whether it be from the ground up or by representing a company's product, is at the heart of direct selling and it is people who made (and continue to make) direct selling the successful marketplace that it is today.

The direct selling marketplace is comprised of *mission-driven* and *socially responsible* companies offering a wide variety of product and services, and the list of direct selling companies is abundant with **entrepreneurs** who built their businesses by utilizing an independent salesforce channel to market and sell their products or services directly to consumers. Possibly one of the most prominent of these entrepreneurs is Mary Kay Ash, a legend as a glass-ceiling breaker and a woman who built a very successful business with a go-to-market strategy of direct selling.

Unlike Mary Kay Ash, however, not all aspiring business owners are willing/able to invest their savings and time on a start-up business. These **micro-entrepreneurs** desire to have the *economic and social benefits* of managing their own businesses but do not want the start-up costs and demands associated with traditional business planning. As such, becoming a **direct selling distributor** offers a low-risk, low-cost pathway to *micro-entrepreneurship*. The traditional barriers to small business ownership are removed when a micro-entrepreneur builds a direct selling business that is backed by established brands. These established brands, several of which are featured in this book, offer the micro-entrepreneurs quality products, business training, and technological resources to achieve a self-determined metric of success.

Framed within the context of *entrepreneurship* and an historical overview of the long-term *sustainability* of this business model, this book is intended for **practitioners** who want to read about the breadth and depth of direct selling. Importantly, this book provides considerable depth in terms of three particular issues associated with direct selling:

- Compensation;
- Ethics and compliance; and
- Global reach.

For **scholars**, this book is built on a strong foundation of valid and reliable research endeavors. The authors have published research on direct selling in high quality, reputable, and peer-reviewed *academic and practitioner journals*. Thus, this book can add foundationally to the research efforts of **academics** who are conducting research in a wide variety of topics (such as *sales, women empowerment, business strategy, ethics, distribution models, gig economy*, and *global entry*—to name a few), as well as to **members of the press** who want reliable and valid content upon which to build their stories. The book's content is also particularly informative for **policy makers** at the local, state, national, and international levels. For **students**, reading this book will offer a variety of insights, particularly related to the intricacies of *channel selection and design.*

Direct Selling: A Global and Social Business Model is a collective project from eight academics and practitioners who have dedicated much of their careers to understanding direct selling as both a go-to-market strategy and a channel of distribution and to capturing the people who are the foundation of direct selling. The pages of this book bring together a wealth of research and knowledge that can inform a broad spectrum of constituents about the *economic and social benefits* of direct selling, while also providing detail and clarity on key issues related to direct selling as a *sustainable business model.*

Keywords

direct selling; social selling; empowering people; business model; channel of distribution; gig economy; independent contractors; micro-entrepreneurs; entrepreneurial spirit; compensation plans; ethics and compliance; go-to-market strategy; high tech—high touch; code of ethics; self-efficacy; B2C marketplace; economic and social benefits

Contents

Testimonials

"This book is a must read for anyone curious about, interested in, or involved with the direct selling channel. The topics are covered thoroughly, and the material is easy to understand. As a lawyer with 30 years of experience in the direct selling marketplace and a former board member of the Direct Selling Education Foundation, I have relied on a variety of materials to explain the ins and outs of direct selling. This excellent book—written by experienced and knowledgeable academics and business leaders—is exactly what I have sought all these years!"—**Kerry Tassopoulos, The Tassopoulos Law Firm PLLC**

"Direct Selling: A Global and Social Business Model is not your typical attempt at a template/process manual to build a business with direct selling as a go-to-market strategy or to become an independent contractor. Rather, this valuable resource brings the reader into the direct selling landscape by bridging the science, art, and heart of the business model. With data, examples, and insights to detail the why, what, and how, you will walk away with great clarity and relational context for engaging in this dynamic marketplace. You will discover why relationships matter and how you, whether the company founder or an independent contractor, have the power to create opportunity and purpose that galvanizes others for measurable social, economic, and global impact."—**Connie Tang, Founder and CEO, Gritty Executive Consulting, LLC; Author—*Fearless Living: 8 Life-Changing Values for Breakthrough Success***

"Given its importance, the direct selling industry has received relatively little research attention. Worse, the industry is often underappreciated and misunderstood! Consequently, this book is long overdue! Top experts in the field have come together to offer different perspectives, ranging from the historic roots to the effects of e-commerce on direct selling. The knowledge, insights, and very accessible style of the authors make this book a true gem and an absolute "must read" for everyone with an interest in direct selling."—**Prof. Bodo B. Schlegelmilch, WU Vienna**

"Direct Selling: A Global and Social Business Model takes us on a long over-due and enlightening journey through the world of direct selling. Bringing academics and practitioners together with an historical and a global per-spective, this book is far more than a "how to" manual of channel tactics—it is an investigation of how direct selling is woven through the global econ-omy. From empowering micro-entrepreneurship to international regulatory compliance, community ties and social ethics to the digital revolution, no stone is left unturned."—**Adam Mills, Loyola University New Orleans**

"Direct selling as a business model and a channel of distribution has defi-nitely fully come into its own as a convenient, personalized, and efficient means of exchange as well as a vital entrepreneurial business model. These authors provide an impressive fact-based and well-balanced treatment of the direct selling opportunity. Painting from different palettes, based on their very diverse backgrounds and areas of expertise, the authors combine to provide definitive coverage of the history, current landscape, broad impact, and future opportunities for direct selling to continue to evolve and thrive. The result is a clear roadmap for how direct selling will add future value to countless entrepreneurially inclined individuals around the world who want to work independently to build a successful business."—**Greg W. Marshall, Rollins College, USA, Aston Business School UK**

"This is an important and timely book for everyone interested in business, micro-entrepreneurship, and the convergence of high-touch and high-tech in marketing products and services. Recent global challenges have accelerated sig-nificant shifts already underway in the direct selling space. The proliferation of technology and an evolution in how we approach our working lives have created an important moment of opportunity for forward-looking entrepre-neurs and companies in the channel. This distinguished group of academic and thought leaders paints a very compelling picture of the proud past and promising future of the direct selling channel."—**Gary Huggins, Executive Director, Direct Selling Education Foundation**

"Direct selling makes a huge contribution to the economy in the United States, as well as the global economy. Unfortunately, this contribution is not always

appreciated and, in fact, its economic role is widely misunderstood. This group of distinguished authors has done an excellent job of communicating why and how direct selling is a critical element of sales and marketing and is absolutely essential to the effective functioning of economic systems around the world. The book combines prophetic brilliance and clarity that informs readers about the foundations and benefits of direct selling in the global economy, as well as to society in general. In so doing, the authors have provided a great service to the economic landscape and the global business environment, and this book should be required reading for all undergraduate and graduate students, particularly business students."—**Joe F. Hair, Jr., Mitchell College of Business, University of South Alabama**

"The past, present, and future of direct selling is presented clearly and with style in Direct Selling: A Global and Social Business Model. The authors understand and respect the opportunities that direct selling has created for entrepreneurs, specifically women, in the 21st century. This book will increase your understanding of the challenges and successes of direct selling across the globe. Specifically, chapters on compensation, compliance, and benefits of direct selling in the gig economy shed light on the success of this often-overlooked go-to-market strategy. If you have a product that you are hoping to take to market, this book may introduce you to a salesforce that will connect with real consumers where they live, spend, and sell."—**Kate Franklin, Director of Wine Guide Success and Happiness, Traveling Vineyard**

*"To best understand a channel of distribution experiencing innovation, transformation, and repositioning, we benefit from **looking back as we look forward**. This book provides the reader with an opportunity to **do both**. I found every chapter to be supportive of critical and strategic thinking. With the growing appeal of the gig-focused economy and the use of technology and digital platforms, the direct seller is envisioned to become even more unique as an intermediary connecting products and services with consumers in a personal manner. Every direct selling company executive needs to understand what is documented and presented in this work."*—**John Fleming, Principal—Ideas & Design Group, LLC; Project Lead/Author— *Ultimate Gig***

"Direct selling has been in practice since the days of the Silk Road. The concept has evolved and become a common part of millions of households around the world. The nature of direct-to-consumer sales allows for the building of customer relationships, as well as the establishment of brand loyalty. Whether it is common knowledge or not, sales skills are heavily utilized in everyday life and engaging in direct selling can further the development of those skills."
—**Helen Brown, Academic Outreach Manager, Vector Marketing**

Foreword

The direct selling channel—defined as a go-to-market strategy that provides brands with high-touch, one-to-one, relationship-driven connections with its customers—is uniquely distinct from traditional and online retail.

Understanding direct selling today requires an appreciation for our history; we are far bigger than an alternative channel of distribution or go-to-market strategy one might encounter in a college textbook. Indeed, we represent a spirit of innovation, and we are powered by an individual's desire to work independently to find the fulfilling social connection one gains when sharing beloved products with others.

The elements that combine to produce a name are often rooted in history, and what we know today as "direct selling" is—in large part—a reflection of the American spirit of individuality and independence that resonates globally.

After the Civil War ravaged the South, many young men, unable to afford higher education, began selling Bibles door-to-door. Just before World War I, and upon recognizing their shared use of "sales agents" to sell products, 10 companies joined together to form the Agents Credit Association—the Direct Selling Association's predecessor—to fight for the interests of the 93,000 traveling salesmen across the United States.

The Great Depression and World War that followed tempered a generation of resilient individuals who would become the founders of direct selling companies that continue today. The postwar boom created opportunities for American women seeking new ways to contribute to their family's financial security.

Across these decades, companies that have chosen to distribute products and services through a direct, person-to-person exchange have come to call themselves direct sellers. Just as direct selling has endured across the decades, the names people have used—and continue to use—to describe their involvement in the channel have evolved in a parallel fashion.

Members of our global community have many names. Some call themselves social sellers. Many may call themselves party plan consultants. Still, others describe themselves as door-to-door, even person-to-person distributors who sell big-ticket products to trusting consumers who maintain fierce loyalty to beloved brands and products.

But no matter the name, the direct selling's dynamism—an engine of self-rejuvenation fueled by its ongoing need to reposition itself to compete in an evolving global marketplace—remains a constant factor in driving the evolution of direct selling worldwide.

Importantly, those calling themselves "direct sellers" share a commitment to ensuring the most ethically rigorous business practices and vigilance for protecting the consumers who participate in the opportunities they create, as well as any consumer who purchases their products.

All embrace the Direct Selling Association (DSA) Code of Ethics as the benchmark for setting bad actors apart from the visionaries whose ideas have empowered millions to start their own direct selling businesses and build better lives for themselves and their families.

In the United States, the DSA is the national trade association for companies that market products and services directly to consumers through an independent, entrepreneurial salesforce known as the direct selling channel.

DSA's mission is to promote, protect, and police the direct selling industry while helping direct selling companies and their independent salesforce become more successful.

DSA's education initiatives ensure that channel leaders have the latest insights and best practices to achieve the high standards of business ethics set by the Association. In 2019, DSA joined with the Better Business Bureau National Programs (BBBNP) to create the Direct Selling Self-Regulatory Council (DSSRC), an independent, impartial monitoring, dispute resolution, and enforcement of false product claims and income representations made by direct selling companies and their salesforce members across digital platforms, regardless of DSA membership.

The World Federation of Direct Selling Associations (WFDSA), based in Washington, DC, is an international organization representing the worldwide direct selling industry.

DSA's sister organization, the Direct Selling Education Foundation (DSEF) works to engage, equip, and empower educators to provide students with an accurate understanding of the direct selling channel as a powerful go-to-market strategy, distribution model, and entrepreneurial option.

Through its Fellows program, the DSEF partners with members of the academic community to support research and education programs that expand knowledge and understanding of the fundamental principles of direct selling. The Foundation works with professors in a variety of disciplines to deliver multifaceted programming aimed directly at the contemporary issues facing direct selling companies and consumers in a global marketplace.

I would like to extend DSA's deepest gratitude to our DSEF Fellows, Dr. Victoria L. Crittenden, Babson College, as well as to: Dr. Sara L. Cochran, Indiana University; Dr. Anne T. Coughlan, Northwestern University; Dr. William Crittenden, Northeastern University; Dr. Linda Ferrell, Auburn University; Dr. O.C. Ferrell, Auburn University; and Dr. Robert A. Peterson, The University of Texas at Austin. We thank you and those other leaders who helped contribute to your research.

Most importantly, I know that you will come to realize that the seemingly simple name "direct selling" is filled with historical, cultural, and strategic marketing meaning. You recognize how some of the brightest brands worldwide employ our channel to maximize their competitive market standing.

JOSEPH N. MARIANO
President and CEO
Direct Selling Association
Washington, DC, 2021

Acknowledgments

Writing this book was an opportunity for us to bring together our many years of collective knowledge about direct selling. For decades, we have spoken and written about direct selling, but we had never encapsulated our thoughts and acquired knowledge into a coherent and broad-based discussion about this fascinating entrepreneurial and business strategy. While our individual direct selling passions are diverse, this book's goal is to bring them together into a tessellation of insight into the various aspects and opportunities of direct selling.

It would be impossible to acknowledge all of the people and companies who have contributed to our understanding and love of direct selling. It is fair to say, however, that this book would not have been possible without the support of the Direct Selling Association and the Direct Selling Education Foundation. The professional staffs within each organization have provided immensely to our research, teaching, and professional activities over the years. Additionally, we offer our sincere gratitude to the direct selling executives and distributors who have contributed to our understanding of direct selling, both over the years and for this book.

In appreciation for all of the contributions (scholarly research, practitioner research, cases, and speaker engagements) made by our fellow academics toward a better understanding of direct selling, we dedicate this book to the Academic Fellows of the Direct Selling Education Foundation.

Introduction

Retail sales of direct selling companies in the United States approximated slightly over US$35 billion in 2019. Globally, retail sales in 2019 were around US$180 billion, generated by almost 120 million independent contractors. Direct selling is a retail business model that markets various types of goods and services such as wellness, home and family care, personal care, clothing and accessories, and leisure and educational offerings. While direct selling enables consumers the benefits of a variety of offerings, there is more to direct selling than consumption and retailing. Direct selling provides an opportunity for entrepreneurially minded individuals to work independently to build a business. Unlike more traditional entrepreneurial start-ups, the direct selling micro-entrepreneur has low start-up and overhead costs since the direct seller is backed by established brands that essentially provide a business-in-a-box comprised of quality products, marketing tools, business training, and technological resources.

While direct selling has been practiced since the mid- to late-1800s, information about the business model is limited in terms of providing a comprehensive understanding of its key components. Thus, the intent of this book is to capture component parts in an easily consumable format compiled by both scholars and practitioners who have spent numerous years understanding and assisting in the growth and development of the direct selling business model. This book takes the reader through the entrepreneurial and historical underpinnings of the business model and then moves to an intensive treatment of compensation and ethics/compliance in direct selling. From there, the book provides a look at the importance and impact of direct selling in the global marketplace and the benefits of direct selling to consumers, participants, and the larger economy. Wrapping up, the book offers a front row seat to the opportunities and challenges in direct selling based on interviews with executives of prominent direct selling companies.

The overarching goal of this book is to educate the reader on the valuable and sensible role that direct selling plays for the individual direct selling companies, the distributor participants, and the society as a whole. For the company, direct selling is a sensible way to approach many geographic and product markets. For the distributor participants, direct selling is an option for entrepreneurial development, income, and social interaction. Societally, the economic impact of direct selling affects the economy as a whole and the social impact of direct selling assimilates into both professional and personal life skills of the direct selling participants.

CHAPTER 1

Entrepreneurial Underpinnings of Direct Selling

Sara L. Cochran

Retail sales of direct selling companies in the United States approximated slightly over US$35 billion in 2019 (Statista 2020). Globally, retail sales in 2019 were around US$180 billion, generated by almost 120 million independent contractors. Direct selling advocates note the benefits of direct selling for achieving entrepreneurial dreams, with some suggesting that direct selling is a key path to entrepreneurship for individuals who want to build their own business. The direct selling channel is comprised of entrepreneurs in the form of direct selling company founders, as well as micro-entrepreneurs who desire the financial and social benefits of entrepreneurial work without the demands of business planning and growth.

Entrepreneurship

While there are many definitions of entrepreneurship, the underlying characteristic is that entrepreneurship involves creating something new without constraints of current resources (Neck 2018; Burgstone 2012). Thereby, the distinguishing characteristic of an entrepreneur is creating something new (Gartner 1988; Neck 2018). Morris and Kuratko (2020) developed a typology to help understand the types of ventures entrepreneurs create. This typology includes survival ventures, lifestyle ventures, managed growth ventures, and aggressive growth ventures.

Survival ventures provide basic hand-to-mouth existence to the entrepreneur and their family and often come from a place of necessity. This type of business may not be formally registered, exists to provide basic needs, does not have many assets, and may even operate on a cash basis; thus, not leaving much to be reinvested in the venture. An example of this type of venture would be a community member who possesses skills in cleaning and decides to begin cleaning the homes of friends and neighbors to make enough money for survival.

Lifestyle ventures provide a stable income for entrepreneurs. This type of venture typically has just one location or market where it can maintain competitiveness and is likely a home-based business. It may have employees but does not seek to expand or grow, which causes heavy dependence on the owner. A lifestyle venture often has limited integration of technology or innovation, with financing by one's self, family, friends, and/or debt. An example of this type of venture would be a local auto shop that has employees and a stable business model, but the shop owner is not looking to expand to other locations or markets.

Managed growth ventures experience continuous, but controlled, growth by launching new offerings or entering into new markets. These ventures maintain a strong local or regional preference and have ongoing reinvestment into the business. An example of this type of venture would be a marketing agency that operates in one city providing basic marketing tasks but grows by adding other services and expanding to additional cities within the region.

Finally, an *aggressive growth venture* seeks exponential growth, often funded with equity capital, and may even have an initial public offering. This type of venture is often founded by a team of entrepreneurs who seek to transform industries. Examples of this type of venture include companies such as Amazon and Spanx.

Each of the four types of ventures provide value to society, with each playing different roles in the economy and making the portfolio important. "As with a portfolio approach to financial investments, where the investor is encouraged not to put all their money into a single type of investment, society is best served by having a diverse mix of venture types" (Morris and Kuratko 2020, 179). Throughout a diverse portfolio, direct selling shows up in each venture type with direct sellers building their own survival or lifestyle ventures and managed growth and aggressive growth entrepreneurs using direct selling as a go-to-market strategy.

The entrepreneurial world can range from high-growth, venture-backed technology startups to selling personal care or household products to friends and neighbors to providing a service such as driving for Uber. Entrepreneurs are encouraged to pursue the type of venture that serves their financial needs as well as fuels their passions. In today's world, many entrepreneurs opt for short-term or variable commitment work, also known as gig work.

The Gig Economy

The world of gig work is greatly changing our economy and creating a new class of entrepreneurs, resulting in what is referred to as the gig economy (Blacharski 2017). There have long been persons seeking alternative work arrangements and, in recent years, technology has driven the expansion of the gig economy (Fleming 2021; Peterson, Crittenden, and Albaum 2019). Companies such as Uber, Lyft, and Upwork have fueled the expansion of these types of opportunities, making the gig economy more in vogue. However, direct selling has provided this type of entrepreneurial opportunity for many decades.[1] In 2020, data showed that 77 percent of Americans were interested in flexible income-earning opportunities (Direct Selling Association 2020), and the gig economy has grown 40 percent since the turn of the century (Caza 2020). Scholars speculate that, due to economic changes related to COVID-19 (i.e., layoffs, shutdowns, flexible work, massive industry shifts), the gig economy will become even more relevant (Caza 2020).

While there are a number of gig opportunities providing entrepreneurs a lower risk path to business ownership, there is a range of cost and risk with various opportunities. An entrepreneur getting into home rental, for example, would have costs associated with property ownership, maintenance, and insurance with an initial cost of at least US$300,000, while a realtor would need training, materials, and membership fees ranging from US$500 to US$1,000. An entrepreneur driving for a

---

[1] Chapter 2 provides an historical framing of direct selling.

company such as Uber or Lyft would need money for an auto purchase, loan, or lease and would have to cover items such as vehicle maintenance, insurance, and gas, all of which might range from US$20,000 to US$40,000. A direct sales entrepreneur would need a startup kit with an average cost of US$83 (Direct Selling Association 2020). Thus, the low cost and risk associated with direct selling makes it an attractive model for entrepreneurs.[2]

Direct Selling

A direct selling company uses independent salespersons to distribute their products. "Direct selling is defined as a channel of distributions for personally selling products directly to consumers away from a fixed retail location. Direct selling includes sales made through one-on-one demonstrations, a party plan, and other personal contact agreements as well as Internet sales. Direct selling occurs at home, at work, and in other non-store locations" (Peterson et al. 2019, 377). While it has always provided a great opportunity for many independent entrepreneurial salespersons, the independent nature of the opportunity has resulted in direct selling becoming confused occasionally with illegal pyramid schemes (Valentine 1998). The primary difference between an ethical direct selling company and a pyramid scheme will be described further in Chapters 3 and 4.

Direct selling is prevalent throughout our global economies, as shown in Chapter 5, and within various types of entrepreneurial ventures. For entrepreneurs, direct selling offers a pathway to business ownership that can take a variety of forms. While direct selling shows up in any type of entrepreneurial venture, it is very common in lifestyle ventures with someone pursuing a direct selling opportunity as an independent salesperson. However, direct selling is also a go-to-market strategy that creates opportunities for the independent salespersons to become direct sales entrepreneurs.

---

[2] Chapter 6 explores the nonfinancial benefits acquired in the direct selling experience as a part of the larger gig economy.

Direct Selling Provides Pathways in Entrepreneurship

The major entrepreneurial pathways in direct selling include: (1) a go-to-market strategy with managed or aggressive growth ventures, (2) an independent sales opportunity with survival or lifestyle ventures as a side gig or means of extra income, and (3) the direct sales entrepreneur with lifestyle ventures as a full-time income generating and passion fulfilling opportunity. This section describes each of these types of pathways and explores specific examples of entrepreneurs who built their ventures using direct selling as a go-to-market strategy and entrepreneurs who have pursued direct selling business-building opportunities.

Go-to-Market Strategy

Entrepreneurs building their businesses must make determinations about their distribution channel, the channel through which consumers can purchase products. For example, a company that makes cosmetic products the consumer obtains from a mass-market retailer has specifically chosen the retail store as the distribution channel. The company offering a higher-end cosmetics line might utilize a specialty retail establishment as its distribution channel. Mary Kay Ash, however, chose to use a direct selling distribution channel as her go-to-market strategy for her line of cosmetics, with company products available for purchase only via a Mary Kay Independent Beauty Consultant (Crittenden and Crittenden 2004). Thus, the go-to-market strategy, or how to get the products into the hands of the consumer, is a deliberate choice made by an entrepreneurial team.

Two entrepreneurs, Mary Kay Ash and Traci Burton, who built their businesses with direct selling as the go-to-market strategy are profiled here.

Mary Kay Ash.[3] Mary Kay Ash launched Mary Kay Inc. in 1963 to provide a different opportunity for women to be salespersons. She said,

---

[3] Mary Kay Ash was the author of several books (Ash 1984; 1994) and much has been written about her entrepreneurial prowess.

"My interest in starting Mary Kay Inc. was to offer women opportunities that didn't exist anywhere else" (Ash 1994, 179). This was during a time when women could not get a bank loan without a man's signature, a struggle Mary Kay herself faced when her husband passed away just before the business was set to launch. Mary Kay developed the company around many principles she lived by. These principles are still upheld today, as evidenced by the company's 2019 recognition as one of the world's most reputable employers in the Global Marketplace 100 Study by Reputation Institute (Direct Selling News Staff 2019).

Mary Kay Inc. was founded by a woman entrepreneur during a time in which it was especially challenging for a woman to get access to capital and other resources needed to launch a venture. Because of this, Mary Kay Inc. has long embodied a support for an entrepreneurial spirit and women's empowerment. This was demonstrated as recently as 2019 when Mary Kay Inc., in collaboration with UN agencies, launched the Women's Entrepreneurship Accelerator. This multiyear partnership initiative was designed to inspire, educate, and empower women entrepreneurs around the world. The UN agencies collaborating on this project include UN Women, United Nations Office for Partnerships (UNOP), International Labour Organization (ILO), International Trade Centre (ITC), UN Global Compact (UNGC), and the United Nations Development Programme (UNDP). The program offers a guided digital curriculum, along with in-person training and mentorship, available in six languages in 192 countries. The Accelerator also serves as an advocacy platform for issues facing women entrepreneurs, such as digital literacy and legal reform (Mary Kay Inc. 2019).

Traci Lynn Burton.[4] Dr. Traci Lynn Burton is the founder of Traci Lynn Jewelry, a business she built from an initial US$200 investment to a multimillion dollar company. After spending her life developing entrepreneurial skills and learning about business, Traci Lynn's first full-time entrepreneurial venture was marketing clothing to customers primarily in African American hair salons. While she was able to build a network of direct sellers and see some success with this venture, she quickly realized the issues with keeping an inventory of multiple sizes that selling clothing

---

[4] Much of the information is this section is derived from Glackin (2019).

presented. Because of this interest in the fashion industry, she pivoted to jewelry to reduce inventory challenges and still serve customers in a similar fashion. She originally built Traci Lynn Jewelry as a franchise model, but she eventually stepped away from the company to be a motivational speaker.

In 2006, Traci Lynn was ready for a change and wanted to find a business to support women. She relaunched Traci Lynn Jewelry and engaged direct sellers via survival and lifestyle ventures to distribute her jewelry and handbag lines. Traci Lynn Jewelry's mission is: "...to provide high-quality affordable fashion jewelry. To create an opportunity for women to start their own business and experience financial freedom" (Glackin 2019, 15). The company's vision is, "...to be our customer's first and best choice for high quality affordable accessories. We will become the leader in the jewelry industry. Our customer's needs will continue to guide our path" (Glackin 2019, 15).

Both Mary Kay Ash and Traci Lynn Burton have received accolades for their entrepreneurial successes. They are just two examples of the many, many successful entrepreneurs who have developed managed growth and aggressive growth companies utilizing a direct sales channel of distribution. Direct selling as a go-to-market strategy not only enables a business model for entrepreneurs, it also affords independent sales opportunities for entrepreneurs to create lifestyle ventures and survival ventures.

Independent Sales Opportunity

In 2017, there were 9.5 million active direct selling participants (Direct Selling Association 2017), with one in 13 adults over the age of 18 in the United States having participated in direct selling as a customer or distributor during their lifetime (DeLiema, Shadel, Nofziger, and Pak 2018). A profile of direct sellers shows that about 50 percent are between the ages of 18 to 25, they are more likely to be female, many have attended at least some college, and the race demographic is similar to that of the race demographic of the United States population (DeLiema et al. 2018). These independent salespersons have a variety of motivations for participating. Figure 1.1 provides a look at the motivations for entering and continuing to stay involved in direct selling.

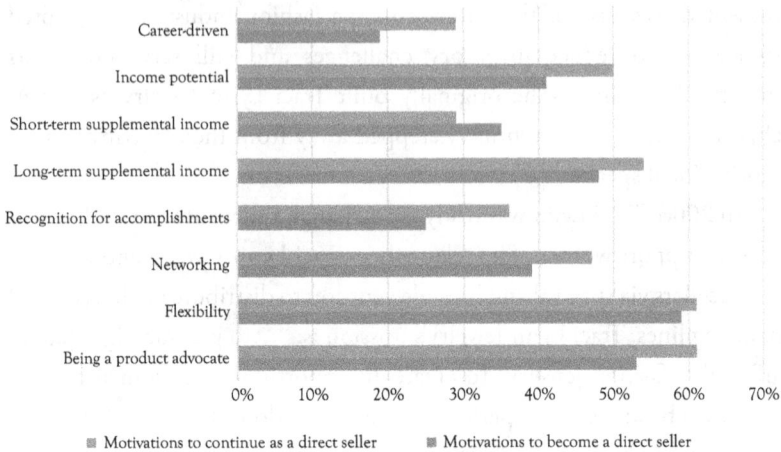

Figure 1.1 *Motivations for becoming and staying involved in direct selling*

Source: Direct Selling Association (2019).

For many, direct selling is a side gig as direct sellers report that they work an average of 13.3 hours per week on their business (DeLiema et al. 2018). The direct selling experience offers both personal and professional benefits as will be seen in more detail in Chapter 6. These benefits include: acquiring better sales skills, believing one could undertake more initiatives, enhancing critical thinking ability, becoming better at coping with and managing stress, becoming better at problem solving, feeling more at ease in front of an audience, enhancing time management skills, improving decision-making skills, and becoming better at managing finances (Peterson et al. 2019).

The result of this array of benefits leaves direct sellers fulfilled with the work. As one direct seller said, "My experience as a woman who has a side job is very empowering. I do not have to rely on anyone else to help me with my bills, I am fully self-supporting and independent, which is an amazing feeling" (King 2018, para. 7). In addition to these skill benefits, 60 percent of direct sellers also report using the extra income to pay for "household needs" such as mortgage or rent, transportation, and food costs (King 2018). There are many opportunities to become an independent business owner, with direct selling companies offering products and services in the following categories: clothing and accessories, cosmetics and personal care, home care, household goods and durables, wellness, books/toys/stationery/and so on, foodstuff and beverages, home improvement, utilities, and financial services (World Federation of Direct Selling Associations 2020).

The following two company examples depict the independent sales opportunity offered by engaging in direct selling.

CUTCO Cutlery/Vector Marketing. CUTCO Cutlery Corp. was formed in 1949 when Alcoa Corp. and W.R. Case & Sons Cutlery Co. formed a joint venture creating high-quality cutlery utilizing a direct selling channel of distribution. Today, CUTCO is a nationally recognized brand, known for high-quality, American-made products with a "forever guarantee" (Ferrell, Ferrell, and Carraway n.d.). Vector Marketing Corporation, a wholly owned subsidiary of the CUTCO Corporation, is the direct sales firm that markets CUTCO products.

Sales representatives begin at Vector Marketing Corporation without having to buy any inventory or samples. The sales representatives start with a commission guarantee of a minimum rate for each demonstration with a potential customer or a weekly commission on actual sales, whichever is higher. The sales opportunity with Vector Marketing allows for increasing commissions based on career sales.

Beyond the initial sales representative opportunity, there are opportunities for some sales representatives to be selected to attend the leadership academy and move into sales leadership roles with the company (e.g., assistant manager, branch manager, district manager). When in these types of leadership roles, managers earn commissions based on the sales of the team members they recruit, train, and motivate. These leadership opportunities enable entrepreneurial salespersons to begin to build their own small businesses within the CUTCO/Vector business model as depicted in this chapter.

Vector Marketing Corporation's sales force is comprised largely of college students from campuses across the United States. The Vector experience provides opportunities for college-age students looking to earn extra money and learn skills such as time management, sales techniques, and personal connection building. Since no previous sales experience is required for an entry-level sales role at Vector Marketing and the company provides sales training, many college students find the opportunity appealing because the experience helps them build their resumes.

Mary Kay Inc.[5] To become a Mary Kay Independent Beauty Consultant (IBC), an individual must submit a signed beauty consultant agreement and purchase a starter kit. This starter kit, with an economic value greater than the kit purchase price, includes full-size products and plenty of business supplies to get started as an IBC. Each IBC is an independent contractor and is encouraged to provide demonstrations of the products during skincare classes. Product inventory is not required to start or maintain a Mary Kay business.

In addition to the commission income generated from personal sales of Mary Kay products, there are opportunities to earn incentives for sales in the form of jewelry, cars, trips, and bonus checks. Additionally, if it aligns with their personal business goals, IBCs can also recruit other IBCs onto their team. Therefore, in addition to earning income on personal sales, IBCs can earn commission based on the production of personal team members.

Creating a culture of recognition for achievement, Mary Kay Inc. holds an annual convention ("Seminar") where independent sales force members are recognized publicly and incentives are awarded to top IBCs. The convention is also full of sessions led by top IBCs providing advice and suggestions on building and growing an independent Mary Kay business for those IBCs who are interested in growing as direct sales entrepreneurs.

Direct Sales Entrepreneur

The direct selling opportunity is also an option for people interested in building survival and lifestyle ventures. These direct selling ventures provide an opportunity for entrepreneurs to experience business ownership in a low-risk, low-cost way by providing resources, training, marketing materials, and personal development opportunities (Crittenden and Bliton 2019). In the examples that follow, we explore how two people took the independent sales opportunities offered by CUTCO/Vector and Mary Kay Inc. and became direct sales entrepreneurs.

---

[5] Information derived from Cochran (2021).

A CUTCO/Vector direct sales entrepreneur.[6] In 2019, a student at Indiana University was studying graphic design, with a minor in entrepreneurship and aspirations of owning her own graphic design business. Knowing she wanted to be an entrepreneur, she knew she had to be able to sell herself and sell her service. She was seeking a summer internship in sales, feeling it would give her useful experience toward her entrepreneurial aspirations. After applying for several internships with no luck, she received a text message saying that someone had recommended her for a sales position with Vector Marketing Corporation. She later found out that her referral was generated through a social media contact, someone she had never met personally. This is a common type of connection given the types of resources and social networking often leveraged by entrepreneurs.

This student pursued the opportunity, beginning as a sales representative going into people's homes and demonstrating the CUTCO line of products. In the fall of that year, she was accepted into the leadership academy and became an assistant manager in a local office. A few months later, she became a branch manager, and, in September 2020, she was promoted to district manager. As the district manager, she is responsible for the team—recruiting and interviewing team members, running meetings, training sales representatives, and helping her team with their daily and weekly tasks. Her compensation is commissions based on her team's sales. She runs her own business as an authorized District Manager for Vector Marketing Corporation.

Through her time with Vector Marketing, the student has learned numerous skills, gained confidence, and developed her resume. She has learned how to work major events with large crowds, designed social media campaigns that can go in her portfolio, interviewed and trained hundreds of young people, managed staff, and had fun running her own business. She is an entrepreneur navigating every aspect of the business. While she does not have any immediate plans to leave her position with Vector Marketing, she knows she would have tremendous opportunities

---

[6] Information derived from personal interview with student.

elsewhere because of the experiences and confidence she has gained through her entrepreneurial journey with Vector Marketing Corporation.

When asked about her proudest moment along this journey, she said that her team was the top new district for the Midwest Region in 2020. However, when she was hosting a team gathering and looking around at everyone having such a good time, she thought to herself, "look at all of these people, having such a great time. I created this." Realizing that her team was getting so much out of the experience that she helped create is now one of her proudest moments with the company.

A Mary Kay Inc. direct sales entrepreneur.[7] In 1995, a long-time consumer of Mary Kay products became frustrated with the school system for which she worked, causing her to explore additional ways to earn money. After researching at-home business models that just did not seem like a good fit, she decided she could at least have a conversation with her Mary Kay Independent Beauty Consultant (IBC) and learn about the opportunity with Mary Kay Inc. Having been a loyal customer for many years, she thought she knew a lot about the company, but she was surprised when she learned about the specifics of being an IBC. She found the potential commission on product retail sales appealing and was further intrigued by the growth opportunities. Importantly, she liked that she could go at her own pace and achieve success without the traditional limits. At that time, she became an IBC, in addition to teaching elementary music full-time and supporting her sons in their activities.

When she began her Mary Kay business, her husband and her mother said, "You're not quitting your day job, right?!" Of course, she said no and assured them she would continue teaching. Much like many entrepreneurs, she first turned to friends and family as she built her business. She continued to build the business and, after just one year, she earned the use of her first career car, quickly followed by earning her first diamond ring.

As she continued to see success with her Mary Kay business and feeling less satisfied with her teaching job, she weighed her options. She was enjoying the mentorship through Mary Kay Inc., as well as the opportunity to earn incentives and feel appreciated. In May 1997, she made

---

[7] Information derived from Cochran (2021).

the decision that she would not return to teaching in the fall term and would focus on her Mary Kay business full-time. Over 25 years later, she had earned the use of 14 company cars, including eight pink Cadillacs, been in the Queen's Court of Sales 24 years with personal retail sales of over US$40,000 each year, and earned an exclusive diamond ring each of those 24 years. Additionally, she was in the Queen's Court of Sharing five times for sponsoring at least 24 personal team members in a year and she earned a diamond bumblebee each time. In addition to personal achievements, her unit was in the Circle of Achievement 18 times for selling over US$300,000 in retail sales in a year and because of these achievements, she earned the Double Star Status 12 times and the Triple Star Status 5 times.

According to this direct sales entrepreneur, her greatest personal accomplishment was being selected as the "Miss Go Give" for March 2015. Each year, 12 independent sales directors are selected by peers for touching their lives and giving without the thought of reciprocation. She says this will forever live as one of her greatest joys.

Conclusion

Direct selling and entrepreneurship form a natural symbiotic relationship. Entrepreneurs need direct selling to build all types of ventures: survival, lifestyle, managed growth, and even aggressive growth. There are examples such as Mary Kay Ash of Mary Kay Inc. and Traci Lynn Burton of Traci Lynn Jewelry who have built companies using the direct selling channel to distribute their products. These companies that use direct selling as the channel of distribution then create individual sales opportunities for those interested in engaging in the gig economy. From this gig work, with a desire to earn extra money, can arise direct sales entrepreneurs who use direct selling to build their own businesses. These direct sales entrepreneurs are backed by established brands comprised of quality products, marketing tools, business training, and technological resources.

In this book, you will read about some of the critical areas in direct selling in the 21st century. Laying the groundwork for understanding these critical areas, Chapter 2 provides an historical perspective on direct selling. Chapters 3, 4, and 5 then focus on the topics of compensation, ethics and compliance, and globalization. Chapter 6 provides an overall look at the benefits afforded by the direct selling opportunity. Finally, Chapter 7 explores the opportunities and challenges in the direct selling marketplace.

References

Ash, M.K. 1984. *Mary Kay on People Management.* New York, NY: Grand Central Pub.

Ash, M.K. 1994. *Miracles Happen: The Life and Timeless Principles of the Founder of Mary Kay Inc.* New York, NY: Harper Collins Publishers.

Blacharski, D. 2017. "Gig Economy Platforms are Creating a New Class of Entrepreneurs." *Entrepreneur.* https://entrepreneur.com/article/288178 (accessed February 18, 2021).

Burgstone, J. 2012. *Breakthrough Entrepreneurship: The Proven Framework for Building Brilliant New Ventures.* San Francisco: Farallon Publishing.

Caza, A. 2020. "The Gig Economy's Implications for Management Education." *Journal of Management Education* 44, no. 5, pp. 594–604.

Cochran, S.L. 2021. "Direct Selling as a Path to Business Ownership: Molly's Mary Kay Journey." *Entrepreneurship Education and Pedagogy* 4, no. 3, pp. 515–526.

Crittenden, V.L., and K. Bliton. 2019. "Direct Selling: The Power of Women Helping Women," In *Go-to-Market Strategies for Women Entrepreneurs*, ed. V.L. Crittenden, 196–205. Bingley, UK: Emerald Publishing.

Crittenden, V.L., and W.F. Crittenden. 2004. "Developing the Sales Force, Growing the Business: The Direct Selling Experience," *Business Horizons* 47, no. 5, pp. 39–44.

DeLiema, M., D. Shadel, A. Nofziger, and K. Pak. 2018. "AARP Study of Multilevel Marketing: Profiling Participants and their Experiences in Direct Sales." https://aarp.org/content/dam/aarp/aarp_foundation/2018/pdf/AARP%20Foundation%20MLM%20Research%20Study%20Report%2010.8.18.pdf (accessed February 18, 2021).

Direct Selling Association. 2017. "Direct Selling in the United States: 2017 Facts and Data." https://dsa.org/docs/default-source/research/dsa_2017_facts anddata_2018.pdf (accessed February 18, 2021).

Direct Selling Association. 2019. "In Direct Selling, Success is Different for Different People."https://dsa.org/docs/default-source/advocacy/dsa-successis differentfactsheetv4.pdf?sfvrsn=2 (accessed February 18, 2021).

Direct Selling Association. 2020. "2020 Consumer Attitudes & Entrepreneurship Study." https://dsa.org/docs/default-source/research/dsa-ipsos-2020-consumerattitudesinfographic2-27.pdf?sfvrsn=68ddfa5_2 (accessed February 18, 2021).

Direct Selling News Staff. 2019. "Mary Kay Inc. Named Among most Reputable Global Employers." *Direct Selling News*, https://directsellingnews.com/mary-kay-inc-named-among-most-reputable-global-employers/ (accessed February 18, 2021).

Ferrell, O.C., L. Ferrell, and D. Carraway. n.d. "Cutting Edge Quality: Cutco Knives for Life." DSEF Case Study (12.1). https://dsef.org/wp-content/uploads/2019/03/DSEF_CS-CutcoV3_031119.pdf (accessed February 18, 2021).

Fleming, J.T. 2021. *Ultimate Gig: Flexibility, Freedom, Rewards.* Bingley, UK: Emerald Publishing.

Gartner, W.B. 1988. "'Who is an Entrepreneur?' is the Wrong Question," *American Journal of Small Business* 12, no. 4, pp. 11–32.

Glackin, C.E. 2019. "Traci Lynn Jewelry: An Entrepreneur Maximizing Shining Opportunities." *The CASE Journal* 15, no. 5, pp. 378–396.

King, R. 2018. "Women love the Flexibility of their Side Hustle – But still Face Unequal Pay." *Gig Employer Blog*, https://fisherphillips.com/gig-employer/tag/gender (accessed February 23, 2021).

Mary Kay Inc. 2019. "Mary Kay, In Collaboration with UN Agencies, Launches Women's Entrepreneurship Accelerator." https://newsroom.marykay.com/en/releases/mary-kay-in-collaboration-with-un-agencies-launches-womens-entrepreneurship-accelerator (accessed February 18, 2021).

Morris, H.H., and D.F. Kuratko. 2020. *What do Entrepreneurs Create? Understanding Four Types of Ventures.* Northampton, MA: Elgar Publishing.

Neck, H.M., C.P. Neck, and E.L. Murray. 2018. *Entrepreneurship: The Practice and Mindset.* Los Angeles, CA: Sage.

Peterson, R.A., V.L. Crittenden, and G. Albaum. 2019. "On the Economic and Social Benefits of Direct Selling," *Business Horizons* 62, pp. 373–382.

Statista. 2020. "Direct Selling Retail Sales in the United States from 2011 to 2019." https://statista.com/statistics/874692/direct-selling-retail-sales-us/ (accessed February 18, 2021).

Valentine, D.A. 1998. "International Monetary Funds Seminar on Current Legal Issues Affecting Central Banks." *Federal Trade Commission*, https://ftc.gov/public-statements/1998/05/pyramid-schemes (accessed February 18, 2021).

World Federation of Direct Selling Associations. 2020. "Global Direct Selling—2019 Retail Sales." https://wfdsa.org/wp-content/uploads/2020/07/Sales-Seller-2020-Report-Final.pdf (accessed February 13, 2021).

CHAPTER 2

Direct Selling—From Camels to Cyberspace

W. Alan Luce and Victoria L. Crittenden

Any social setting can be read as a historical document of itself shelved momentarily between past and present. Whatever the current social order, we know it became from what it was in the past. To where the social order evolves, we know it will arrive there by some transformation of what it is now.

(Barley 1990, 222)

On just about any day or night 6,000 years ago, before the development of writing and before the zero was invented that would lead to the development of modern math, you would find men trudging along, leading and sometimes riding their camels. Traveling along what became known as the "Silk Road," they moved trade goods from China and India in the east to the burgeoning civilizations in Egypt and in Mesopotamia empires such as Babylon and Assyria. These early entrepreneurs had figured out that they could buy goods in the local markets, where items such as silk and spices were plentiful and relatively cheap, and take these goods west to Mesopotamia where the same items were rare and highly sought after. There, they could trade the items for a profit.

As time passed, the role of the peddler evolved into a way for hard-to-obtain goods (e.g., blades, tools, fabrics, spices, and salt) to be distributed in small villages, country estates, and fortresses of the aristocracy. Large quantities of these goods came into ports such as London or Amsterdam and were taken to the weekly public markets to be sold to the local population. The public markets worked fine for city dwellers, but these items were also needed by rural folks spread about the countryside in villages and shires well away from the ports. Once again, the entrepreneurial peddlers (or "chapmen" according to Brodie 1999) saw an opportunity and filled an important product distribution role. Loading up in the ports and city centers where the goods were relatively cheap, the peddlers took their carts of goods into the countryside to bring these hard-to-obtain items to anxious buyers. When a peddler came into a village, he was welcomed. In addition to goods, the peddler brought news of the outside world. In return for a place to sleep and free meals, the peddler would entertain the town with his stories and news. In many cases, the first time an isolated village learned that the old king had died and a new king was on the throne was hearing it from one of these traveling peddlers.

Over time, the peddlers came to follow one of two commercial strategies. The first was to take basic, necessity goods to the rural villages and shires, often including other services such as blade sharpening and blacksmithing to repair broken tools. The other strategy was to bring high-end luxury goods (e.g., silk, Italian lace, glass items, mirrors, and combs) to wealthy farmers, local aristocracy, and large landholders. This reliance on peddlers to distribute needed necessities and luxury goods out into the countryside continued for more than four millennia.

When European nations started to colonize places like North America, they set the stage for the next big evolution in selling. The French, Dutch, and English settlers brought their customs and cultures with them and, as they expanded inland from the coastal settlements, the peddlers were needed to bring goods and services to the many new inland communities, ranches, and farms. Often known as "Yankee Peddlers," these direct sellers picked up goods at ports and they would then point their carts toward following the trails established by the early settlers to their villages and homesteads. The Yankee Peddlers were fulfilling essentially the same role that their earlier iterations had performed for hundreds of years in the old world.

As depicted in Figure 2.1, these 18th-century Yankee Peddlers set the stage for the direct-to-consumer channel of distribution that we now know as direct selling (Emmert 2014). Schreyögg, Sydow, and Holtmann (2011) refer to the importance of past events when discussing the path dependence or historical conditioning of organizational actions.

This path dependence helps explain how institutional persistence and, oftentimes, puzzling stability have invigorated the direct selling marketplace. This book is a compilation of reflective points about direct selling, and the purpose of this chapter, in the tradition of reflection (Yancey 1998), is to cast backward to understand the evolution of direct selling.

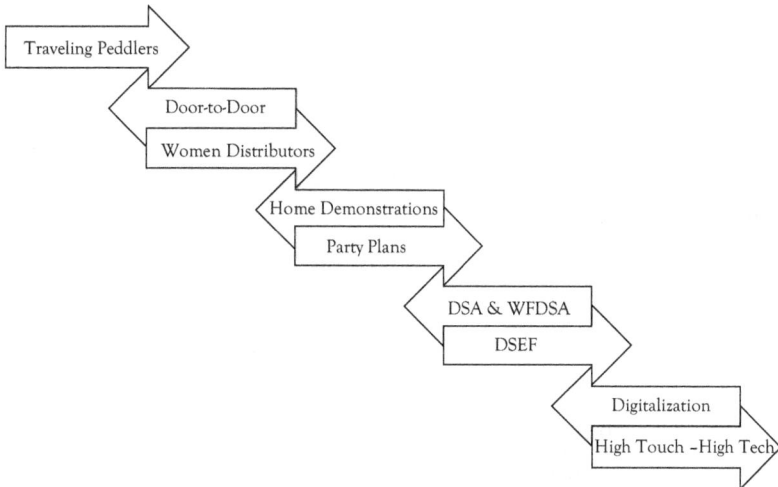

Figure 2.1 The direct selling journey

The Evolution of Direct Selling

Today, a wide variety of consumer goods and services are offered through direct selling. Major product categories include clothing and accessories, cosmetics and personal care, home care, household goods and durables, wellness, books/toys/stationery, foodstuff and beverages, home improvement, utilities, and financial services (World Federation of Direct Selling Associations 2020). Direct selling is a unique retail channel since direct selling companies rely upon a salesforce of independent distributors who earn commissions on sales of a direct selling company's products. The independent distributors are backed by established direct selling companies that provide a "business-in-a-box" comprising quality products, marketing tools, business training, and technological resources (Crittenden and Bliton 2019). All the while, the independent distributors maintain the flexibility of setting their own hours and engaging as much or as little as they desire.

Emmert (2014) refers to the "paradigm-shifting events and thresholds" that helped shape 21st-century direct selling. These events and thresholds are given as follows: (1) the first recognized direct selling company established in 1855 that had young men going door-to-door to sell products, (2) the welcoming of women as distributors, (3) the formation of the Direct Selling Association (DSA), (4) a revolutionary approach for compensation, and (5) the evolution of the sales method. These paradigm-shifting events and thresholds are captured here in a chronological story of direct selling.

Mid-to-Late 1800s

Rev. James Robinson Graves was the forerunner to the direct selling business model that we know today. In 1855, Rev. Graves began sending young men door to door to sell Bibles and educational materials as a means to earn money for going to college (Asenshia 2016). This door-to-door business model formed the basis for the first direct selling company; now known as Southwestern Advantage (originally just "Southwestern"), the company is the oldest direct seller in America. According to the Direct Selling News (2019):

> [the company] helps young people develop the skills and character they need to achieve their goals in life. The independent dealers run a business selling educational products to families to help off-set their educational expenses during their summer break.

Soon to follow Southwestern was the California Perfume Company. David H. McConnell was a traveling book salesman who gave free perfume samples to his customers. As the story goes, he realized that his customers had more interest in the perfume samples than books (Avon 2016). Thus, he began mixing fragrances himself and, having worked with a very successful woman bookseller named Mrs. Persis Foster Eames Albee, Mr. McConnell asked Mrs. Albee to sell his perfumes. Not only was Mrs. Albee the first sales representative for the California Perfume Company, she is also known as the first "Avon Lady" since the California Perfume

Company was renamed Avon in 1939 (Asenshia 2016; Avon 2016). Mr. McConnell made a bold statement for the times when he recruited women as sales representatives, and he set the stage for utilizing the direct selling business model as a means of economic freedom for women.

Early 1900s

In 1906, Sarah Breedlove officially changed her name to Madam C.J. Walker and soon thereafter began selling "Madam Walker's Wonderful Hair Grower." Her customers soon became her "evangelical agents," receiving a commission to sell the products for her (Gates 2013). Madam C.J. Walker was one of the earliest successful African American woman entrepreneurs. While the Walker Manufacturing Company was not necessarily a direct selling company since the focus was more on hair colleges and setting up businesses using the Walker System, Madam C.J. Walker, like Mr. McConnell, showed the power of using a woman's social network to generate business.

Frank Stanley Beveridge was a successful Fuller Brush Company salesperson. His success was attributed to the fact that he demonstrated his products at home parties. That is, a group of people would gather at someone's home, Mr. Beveridge would demonstrate to the group as a whole and then the group would buy en masse. In 1931, Mr. Beveridge opened his own company, Stanley Home Products, using this group home demonstration approach (Asenshia 2016).

Brownie Wise was a Stanley salesperson, but she left the company to go to work for Tupperware. It is at Tupperware where Brownie Wise is credited with creating the party plan model for direct selling (Emmert 2014). The party plan method was just that—a socializing party where Tupperware was sold, with incentives offered to both the selling agent and the party host. The party plan soon became a new norm for the direct selling marketplace (Asenshia 2016). Joining Brownie Wise in the party plan sales model were two other women sales leaders previously with Stanley Home Products: Mary Crowley and Mary Kay Ash. Mary Crowley was founder and CEO of Home Interiors and Gifts, Inc., and Mary Kay Ash founded Mary Kay Cosmetics.

Thus, three women (Brownie Wise, Mary Crowley, and Mary Kay Ash) are responsible for the success of three major direct selling companies in the United States (Tupperware, Home Interiors and Gifts, and Mary Kay Inc.), as well as the evolution and success of the party plan model of direct selling. These three women had a desire to see women succeed and recognized that there was more than financial success. In the words of Ash (1984, 98), "At Mary Kay, we teach people how to spread their wings and fly on their own."[1]

The turn of the century brought with it not only more direct selling companies and the party plan model, but it was also the time for early efforts to align direct selling companies into a cohesive group of companies focusing on the needs of direct sellers. In 1910, the California Perfume Company joined with nine other companies from New York, Massachusetts, and Michigan to form the Agents Credit Association (Emmert 2014). The initial purpose of the association was to help with credit and collection issues (Asenshia 2016).

Mid-to-Late 1900s

The second half of the 20th century was a time when direct selling companies were experiencing a sharp focus on structural issues related to the business model. The Agents Credit Association took on a bigger purpose in terms of creating codes of ethics, advocacy, and consumer protection (Asenshia 2016). The association evolved into the DSA, which is now the national trade association for companies that market products and services directly to consumers through an independent, entrepreneurial salesforce. The DSA's mission is "to protect, serve and promote the effectiveness of member companies and the independent business people they represent. To ensure member companies' products and the direct selling opportunity is conducted with the highest level of business ethics" (Direct Selling Association 2021c).

In 1970 the DSA enacted a Code of Ethics—a robust series of policies that every DSA member agrees to follow (Direct Selling Association 2021a). The Code holds member companies accountable to policies that

---

[1] The nonfinancial benefits of direct selling are discussed further in Chapter 6.

seek to protect both the independent salesperson and the direct selling consumer. With stringent guidelines for earnings representations, product claims, sales and marketing tactics, and policies for order cancellations and returns, the DSA Code of Ethics helps to ensure the integrity of the channel.[2]

Now, in addition to the DSA in the United States, there is also the WFDSA, a nongovernmental, voluntary organization founded in 1978 that represents direct selling globally with over 60 national DSAs and one regional organization, representing direct selling in 170 countries (World Federation of Direct Selling Associations 2020). The regional organization is the Federation of European Direct Selling Associations (SELDIA). The SELDIA, representing all forms of direct selling in Europe, has 23 direct selling member associations in the European Union and 16 corporate member companies (Direct Selling Association 2021b).[3]

In 1973, the Direct Selling Education Foundation (DSEF) was founded by visionaries in the DSA as a Washington, DC-based 501c3 organization, funded by contributions from DSA member companies, suppliers, and individuals. The purpose of the DSEF is to empower educators to provide students with an accurate understanding of direct selling. To accomplish this purpose, the DSEF partners with educators, largely through the DSEF Fellows program that was later created in 2016. This program is a group of over 200 university and community college professors with specialties that fall mainly within the areas of management, marketing, entrepreneurship, ethics, and consumer studies, as well as other related fields (Direct Selling Education Foundation 2020).

In addition to the formation of formal groups of direct selling companies and individuals, a revolutionary approach to compensation was being developed by the mid-1900s. As described previously, the independent contractors in direct selling were compensated using a performance-based model where earnings were tied to personal sales (Emmert 2014). However, direct selling companies had long recognized the power of a salesperson's social network for recruiting others to sell product. Thus, the revolution in the compensation structure was that of awarding

---

[2] More about ethics appears in Chapter 4.
[3] More about direct selling globally appears in Chapter 5.

commissions to salespeople based on individual sales effort as well as commissions on the sales efforts of independent contractors whom a salesperson trained. This change in the compensation structure, implemented first at Nutrilite (which was later acquired by Amway), sparked a decades-long boom for direct selling (Emmert 2014).[4]

As evidenced, the latter half of the 20th century was a busy time for the direct selling marketplace with numerous start-ups, rapid growth among the more established companies, changes to the business model with the party plan approach, modifications to the compensation structure in terms of a salesperson's downline, and formalized governing bodies. However, according to Emmert (2014), "perhaps no event in the history of direct selling has caused more of a paradigm shift than the emergence of technology." The advent of the computer changed everything—from order processing to compensation management to inventory control to customer transaction history to electronic payments—making operational excellence paramount in direct selling companies. From this desire for operational excellence arose a number of niche suppliers that could provide behind-the-scenes technological support. However, technology soon grew beyond meeting the demands of internal operational excellence.

The Technological Unfolding in the 2000s

Direct sellers are in the people business. As portrayed in the historical overview of direct selling, the independent distributor who brings high touch to the sales process has long been key in direct selling. These independent distributors possess extensive knowledge of the product, and their personal interactions with customers (many of whom are friends and family) in the luxury of the customer's home have resulted in a marketplace valued in billions of dollars. However, the start of the 21st century brought with it a technology explosion that enabled new ways of reaching the customer. The digitalization era had begun for direct selling, but as noted by Sheri McCoy at Avon Products, Inc. (Emmert 2014), "While the biggest game changer is technology and how we use it, the backbone of our business hasn't changed. Our representatives continue to

---

[4] More on the downline approach to compensation is in Chapter 3.

build relationships and have a passion for our products, and our business is still high-touch, even though it is now high tech too."

Recognizing that the personal connection with customers was key to success, direct sellers began to align high-tech marketing practices with the traditional high-touch nature of direct selling. For example, Origami Owl had its own media center that offered a single template for independent sales consultants to create, in mere minutes, a personalized brochure that could be printed or shared via a social media link. Rodan + Fields built a robust SoLoMo organization that both empowered the independent sales force and delighted the Rodan + Fields customer. Direct selling giants Avon and Mary Kay created virtual mirrors for customers to try on products in the comfort of their homes at any time day or night—no salesperson presence needed. In the words of Crittenden, Crittenden and Crittenden (2019, 265), "High touch met, and fit with, high tech."

By 2010, direct selling companies had adopted digital tools with companies and independent distributors utilizing social media platforms to engage with customers. Companies were engaging with independent distributors in various ways on owned platforms, and independent distributors were engaging with their customers on social platforms (e.g., Facebook). With that, however, also came the need for new methods of regulation since social media posts with, for example, even subtle suggestions that direct selling could make financial and/or health worries go away could place companies in violation per the Federal Trade Commission (Martin 2019). In 2019, Brett Duncan, cofounder and managing partner of Strategic Choice Partners (a consulting firm that offers strategic support and services to direct selling companies), wrote a brief opinion piece titled "2019: The Year Direct Selling as We Know It Changed Forever." Duncan (2019) identified three market forces: (1) new regulations, (2) the consumer marketplace, and (3) the entrepreneur marketplace.

In terms of new regulations, the DSA created the Direct Selling Self-Regulatory Council (DSSRC) in 2019. The DSSRC is a third-party self-regulatory program administered by BBB National Programs, Inc. (formerly Council of Better Business Bureaus).[5] As far as the consumer

---

[5] More about the DSSRC is available in Chapter 4.

marketplace, Duncan (2019) suggested that the consumer marketplace was changing in areas such as the shopping experience, access (particularly relative to online giants such as Amazon), interaction, and competitive lifespan. The third market force, entrepreneur marketplace, highlighted the fact that direct selling was no longer the only gig in town. With the gig economy growing, as noted in Chapter 1 with more discussion in Chapter 6, direct selling firms were facing competition, not just in terms of consumer selections, but also for the independent distributors that have long been the mainstay of direct selling.

While 2019 might have been a year of change for direct selling, 2020 was a year of challenges (Luce 2020). The negative effects of COVID-19 and the pandemic are long lasting. Death, illness, and job/income loss have had catastrophic effects on millions of people worldwide. Isolation, social distancing, and mask wearing will likely have a cultural impact that changes human behavior as we have known it. The challenges of 2020, however, have led to the three Cs of direct selling in 2021 (Luce 2020): Chance, Change, and Challenges.

The *chance* element (when a vaccine will be available for all, the percentage of the population that will take the vaccine, and the degree of normalcy relative to pre-COVID times) will have a significant impact on sales and inventory forecasts. Interestingly, the *change* element has worked in favor of direct selling. As noted previously, direct selling companies had already adopted technological platforms that enabled the virtual selling events required by the pandemic, and onboarding of independent distributors adapted quickly to the online environment. Job losses resulted in people seeking out work that would help pay the bills. Direct selling has the competitive advantage that it does not require distributors to leave home, since sales engagement can occur virtually and order processing electronically. This offered the added benefit of not having to leave home (unlike Uber drivers, grocery store employees, delivery people, etc.), which meant no childcare was needed and there was no risk of exposure to the virus.

Unfortunately, *challenges* are ahead for direct selling in 2021 and beyond. While the independent distributor has been the mainstay of direct selling, these distributors, who are the ones out in the field engaging with customers, have navigated to online sales events, social media, and digital acquisition tools. Many distributors may have never physically held a particular company's product in their hands or even met face-to-face with a group leader. The independent sales force has now become the online independent sales force. As seen in Chapter 7, company executives feel challenged in building a sense of community and organizational culture in a technological platform world. Additionally, current senior-level sales executives in direct selling companies may be uncertain on how to lead in this new technology-driven environment. As noted in a blog by Rallyware (2020), a company that offers software to direct selling companies, "[digital transformation exacerbated by the pandemic] is a genie that will not go back into the bottle any time soon."

Looking Forward by Casting Backward

This chapter has provided a look at the direct selling journey—a journey from camels on the Silk Road to virtual sales parties in cyberspace. As noted in Chapter 1, direct selling is both a go-to-market strategy and, according to Fleming (2021), one of the first forms of gig work. History shows that it has long been both, with many companies and individuals achieving considerable success in both forms. Just as there have been challenges through the decades, similar challenges lie ahead as will be seen in the remainder of this book. Direct selling companies have evolved over time, becoming what they are today because of transformations that were made over time. They will continue to do so in preparation to take advantage of the opportunities that lie ahead.

References

Asenshia. 2016. "The Roots of Modern Direct Selling." https://asenshia.com/the-roots-of-modern-direct-selling/ (accessed March 25, 2021).

Ash, M.K. 1984. *Mary Kay on People Management.* New York, NY: Grand Central Pub.

Avon. 2016. "Our Story." https://avonworldwide.com/about-us/our-story#:~:text=1939,Perfume%20Company%20is%20renamed%20Avon (accessed March 25, 2021).

Barley, S.R. 1990. "Images of Imaging: Notes on doing Longitudinal Field Work." *Organization Science* 1, no. 3, pp. 220–247.

Brodie, A.S. 1999. *Self-Employment Dynamics of the Independent Contractor in the Direct Selling Industry.* [doctoral dissertation]. University of Westminster. https://westminsterresearch.westminster.ac.uk/download/f5d8a8d91865 fd5158fb325a379fb7d1555b79164bbe6abe47f7e17f5c066781/1085878/ Andrew_Stewart_BRODIE.pdf (accessed March 25, 2021).

Crittenden, V.L., and K.H. Bliton. 2019. "Direct Selling: Women Helping Women." In *Go-to-Market Strategies for Women Entrepreneurs: Creating and Exploring Success,* ed. V.L. Crittenden. Emerald Group Publishing, pp. 195–205.

Crittenden, A.B., V.L. Crittenden, and W.F. Crittenden. 2019. "The Digitalization Triumvirate: How Incumbents Survive." *Business Horizons* 62, no. 2, pp. 259–266.

Direct Selling Association. 2021a. "Code of Ethics." https://dsa.org/ consumerprotection/code-of-ethics (accessed March 26, 2021).

Direct Selling Association. 2021b. "Global Partners." https://dsa.org/about/ globalpartners (accessed March 25, 2021).

Direct Selling Association. 2021c. "Who We Are." https://dsa.org/about/ association (accessed March 25, 2021).

Direct Selling Education Foundation. 2020. "About the Direct Selling Education Foundation." https://dsef.org/direct-selling-education-about/ (accessed March 26, 2021).

Direct Selling News. 2019. "Company Profiles—Southwestern Advantage." https://directsellingnews.com/company-profiles/southwestern-advantage/ (accessed March 25, 2021).

Duncan, B. 2019. "The Year Direct Selling as We Know it Changed Forever." *The World of Direct Selling,* https://worldofdirectselling.com/direct-selling-changed-forever/ (accessed March 26, 2021).

Emmert, J.M. 2014. "The Big History of Direct Selling." *Direct Selling News,* https://directsellingnews.com/the-big-history-of-direct-selling (accessed March 25, 2021).

Fleming, J.T. 2021. *Ultimate Gig: Flexibility, Freedom, Rewards.* Bingley, UK: Emerald Publishing.

Gates, H.L. 2013. "Madame Walker, The First Black American Woman to be a Self-Made Millionaire." https://pbs.org/wnet/african-americans-many-rivers-to-cross/history/100-amazing-facts/madam-walker-the-first-black-american-woman-to-be-a-self-made-millionaire/ (accessed March 25, 2021).

Luce, W.A. 2020. "2021: A Year of Chance, Change, & Challenges." *Direct Selling News,* https://directsellingnews.com/2021-a-year-of-chance-change-challenges/?utm_source=rss&utm_medium=rss&utm_campaign=2021-a-year-of-chance-change-challenges (accessed March 26, 2021).

Martin, H. 2019. "5 Events that Impacted Direct Selling in 2019." *Direct Selling News*, https://directsellingnews.com/5-events-that-impacted-direct-selling-in-2019/ (accessed March 26, 2021).

Rallyware. 2020. "COVID-19 and the Transformation of Direct Selling." https://rallyware.com/blog/covid-19-and-the-transformation-of-direct-selling (accessed March 26, 2021).

Schreyögg, G., J. Sydow, and P. Holtmann. 2011. "How History Matters in Organizations: The Case of Path Dependence." *Management & Organizational History* 6, no. 1, pp. 81–100.

WFDSA. 2020. "2019/2020 Annual Report." https://wfdsa.org/download/advocacy/annual_report/WFDSA-Annual-Report-2020.pdf (accessed March 27, 2021).

World Federation of Direct Selling Associations. 2020. "Global Sales by Product Category." https://wfdsa.org/wp-content/uploads/2020/07/Product-2020-Report-Final.pdf (accessed March 26, 2021).

Yancey, K.B. 1998. *Reflection in the Writing Classroom*. Louisville, Colorado: University Press of Colorado, http://jstore.org/stable/j.ctt46nsh0 (accessed March 25, 2021).

CHAPTER 3

Direct Selling Distributor Compensation Plans

Anne T. Coughlan

A direct selling (DS) firm is defined by the type of distribution channel it creates to take its products from point of production to point of consumption. The DS distribution channel consists of three primary types of channel members: the DS firm itself (similar to a manufacturer in a non-DS channel); a set of independent contractors called distributors[1]; and nondistributor consumers.[2] These channel members are jointly responsible for getting the work of the DS channel done, just as is true in non-DS channels.

The design of any distribution channel, the DS channel included, requires that the work of the channel—that is, the channel's various tasks and activities—be assigned to one or more channel members.[3] A DS channel is captained by the DS firm itself, which chooses the allocation of responsibilities for these channel activities. It assigns the tasks of *retail selling* and *sales recruitment and management* to its distributors.

---

[1] These individuals are sometimes also called "associates" or "consultants."

[2] This chapter refers to the nondistributor end-user as a "consumer," in deference to the prominence of consumer products and services sold using DS channels. Some business-to-business (B2B) sales are also made through DS channels to businesses that are the true end-users of the firm's product. Just two of the multiple such examples are Amway, which sells cleaning products (among many other products) to consumers as well as to businesses (www.amway.com), and LegalShield, a DS company that sells legal coverage to both consumer and business end-users (https://www.legalshield.com/).

[3] See Chapter 2 for a history of DS culminating in today's distribution channel structure and split of channel activities.

It typically carries for itself the responsibilities for product line design, product sourcing and manufacturing, corporate-level warehousing, branding, distributor training and education, consumer service, shipping (to distributors and/or nondistributor consumers), returns management, IT investments, compensation, database management for all distributors, website management (between the firm and its distributors and for distributors to face the market), and other overhead activities such as compliance and legal.

In short, the DS firm relies on members of its distributor force to be its *field sales force* through retail selling efforts, as well as to be the *sales managers* of the channel, through their recruitment, mentoring, and development of other distributors. These are of course crucial activities to the DS firm's health and survival, with sales compensation providing the incentives for distributors to choose to perform the channel functions fully allocated to the distributor force as a whole.

The DS firm thus offers any prospective and all incumbent distributors a complete entrepreneurial opportunity that includes a developed and curated branded product line, with marketing and pricing guidelines, a compensation system to reward a given distributor and any other distributors she may recruit and manage in a "downline," and promotional (including Internet) tools to facilitate the sale of products and the building and mentorship of downlines. In return, the firm allows each distributor to buy and personally consume its products (usually at a discounted wholesale price) and expects the distributor force, as a whole, to act as a *retail sales force*, as well as to carry out *sales management* functions. The very design of the DS channel necessitates a well-designed compensation system if it is to succeed.

Distributor Compensation Plays a Crucial Role in the DS Channel

An effective compensation structure is crucial to the success of any firm's channel, including that of a DS firm, because it is the incentive link from the channel design (which allocates responsibility for various activities to distributors) to effective implementation of that design. While this chapter focuses on compensation structures for DS distribution channels, it is important to recognize the parallel goals of compensation-setting in DS and non-DS channels. Table 3.1 illustrates how the classic non-DS sales force roles of field salesperson, district sales manager, and national sales manager/vice president are similar to those of a retail seller, a business builder, and a leadership team builder in a DS context.

Table 3.1 Non-DS and DS sales force roles and rewards

Non-DS sales force*	DS distributor force
Field salesperson: Responsible for sales generation; rewarded with commissions on own book of sales	Retail seller: Rewarded with retail markup income on own sales, and sometimes with commissions on personal volume
Field/Area/District sales manager, with own book of sales and responsibility for developing team of 10–15 field sales reps: rewarded with commissions on own book of sales, plus commissions/bonuses on team sales	Business builder: Rewarded with retail markup income on own sales, commissions/bonuses on group (own + team) volume
National sales manager, usually little/no book of own sales: Rewarded with commissions/bonuses on overall performance of national sales force, and for leader presence throughout the organization	Leadership team distributor (varying titles at different DS firms): As for Business Builder, but separately rewarded for "breakaway" downline team performance; expected to act as organization leader and motivator

Note: Non-DS sales force members may also be paid a salary, unlike DS distributors.

More generally, the goals of DS distributor compensation include the following:

- To *attract* prospects to enroll as distributors and to *retain* current distributors;
- To *motivate* desired actions and performance levels by each distributor and *motivate* salespeople's overall effort exertion at as high a level as possible;
- To create *aspirational opportunities* for those with a goal to excel on multiple or higher level sales activities; and
- To *demotivate unwanted behaviors*, including poor effort, poor consumer service, poor sales management behaviors, and/or misrepresentations of the firm's products and opportunities.

A well-designed DS distributor compensation plan thus motivates distributors to exert effort toward their two key value-added functions of retail selling and distributor network building and mentorship.

Unlike an employee sales force, a DS distributor force generally consists of a set of *independent contractors*. Typical DS distributor enrollment contract wording[4] describes independent contractor status as follows:

As a distributor you are a self-employed independent contractor. As such, you have complete freedom in determining the number of hours you will devote to your business, the scheduling of such hours, and the investments you will make in running your DS business. The firm will not provide you with a place of business, and if you desire a place of business other than your own residence, you will be responsible for procuring, furnishing, equipping, and paying for it. As an independent contractor, you are not an employee, agent, franchisee, fiduciary, or beneficiary of the company or of any other distributor. You are responsible for all laws applicable to your business, including but not limited to obtaining all necessary licenses, permits, and other government approvals applicable to your business and paying all required taxes. You will not be treated as an employee for federal or state tax purposes, or for purposes of the Federal Unemployment Act, Insurance Contributions Act, or Social Security Act, any state unemployment laws, state employment security laws, or state workers' compensation laws.

The DS firm, therefore, foregoes the ability to supervise or control the independent contractor distributor's time allocation and choice of work activities. Any distributor can decide whether and how much to work on retail selling (if at all) and whether or how much to seek to recruit and mentor downline distributors (if at all). She can choose to work steadily every week, or only sporadically or seasonally throughout the year. She can choose to promote a limited subset of the DS firm's full product line

---

[4] These statements are commonly used in most DS distributor registration agreements, but the wording presented here is not a quotation from any particular DS firm.

or the whole line. The distributor is free *not* to work at any of these activities if she wishes, and, indeed, some distributors enroll solely to be able to buy the firm's products at distributor discounted prices.[5]

As a result, DS distributor compensation is the only real tool at the DS firm's command to influence the distributor to perform the channel activities delegated to the DS distributor force at large. Importantly, successful DS compensation design does not have to motivate *all* distributors to perform *all* designated channel activities *all* the time. However, the compensation plan must succeed in attracting and motivating a distributor force that *overall* performs the desired activities, resulting in robust retail sales and in a vibrant and motivated distributor force.

Because the DS compensation plan must motivate multiple distinct channel activities, it must contain multiple reward components. A simple discount structure allowing retail markup income to be earned on one's own retail sales, for example, would be insufficient to motivate a distributor to find, recruit, and mentor other distributors. As well, the motivation of network building and maintenance must recognize the skill and effort involved in managing a small or a large downline of distributors. The overall compensation plan must reward distributors with different motivations and goals to perform at different levels and must be attractive enough to encourage retention in the distributor force. Finally, the compensation plan must include elements that demotivate any distributor from various undesirable behaviors, such as encouraging downline distributors to load up on inventory or failing to train and support downline distributors.

---

[5] Some DS firms now allow such individuals to enroll as "Preferred Customers," which may entail a lower registration fee, gives the individual access to the firm's product line at a discount, and prevents the individual from engaging in either retail selling or downline network-building activities. Nevertheless, it is generally still possible for an individual to enroll as a full-fledged distributor, yet to choose not to pursue retailing or business-building activities.

The DS's Distributor Compensation Plan
Distinguishes an Illegal Pyramid Scheme
From a Legitimate DS Channel

DS, a legitimate distribution channel, is distinct from—but some-times confused with—an illegal pyramid scheme. The legal distinction between the two rests on the DS distributor compensation structure, highlighting the relevance of this chapter's focus on DS distributor compensation.

Case law and state laws in the United States have established a fairly robust definition of a pyramid scheme. The *Amway* case stated that, "'Pyramid' sales plans involve compensation for recruiting regardless of consumer sales."[6] The *Koscot* case[7] refined and expanded the definition in its description of an illegal pyramid scheme as an "entrepreneurial chain,"

> *characterized by the payment by participants of money to the company in return for which they receive (1) the right to sell a product and (2) the right to receive in return for recruiting other participants into the program rewards which are unrelated to sale of the product to ultimate users...*[8]

Pyramid schemes are regulated by state laws in the United States, which are largely consistent with the above two commentaries. Some define a pyramid scheme as a plan whose enrollee offers a payment (called a "consideration") in order to receive compensation "derived primarily" from recruitment, rather than from product sales. Whether the rewards are completely or "primarily" unrelated to sales, the underlying principle is still that a pyramid scheme awards compensation for mere recruitment,

---

[6] *In the Matter of Amway Corp.*, 93 F.T.C. 618, 1979 FTC LEXIS 390, *97 (F.T.C. 1979).

[7] *In the Matter of Koscot Interplanetary, Inc.*, 86 F.T.C. 1106, 1975 WL 173318, (F.T.C. 1975).

[8] *In the Matter of Koscot Interplanetary, Inc.*, 86 F.T.C. 1106, 1975 WL 173318, p. 49 (F.T.C. 1975).

essentially offering a "headhunter" fee that is not dependent on the retail selling performance by the recruit.[9]

Some question whether personal consumption of the firm's products by distributors themselves are part of "product sales,"[10] although it makes logical sense to count them as true end-user sales, since DS distributors commonly enjoy the products they sell and, therefore, voluntarily consume them after becoming a distributor (just as many did before they enrolled).

In sum, an illegal pyramid scheme is characterized by (a) a payment or consideration offered, and (b) the resulting right not only to sell the firm's products but also to earn compensation based (entirely or mainly) on recruitment without regard to end-user product sales (be the end-user a nondistributor or a distributor). Note that other descriptors, such as the size of the initial enrollment fee, the amount (if any) of inventory a distributor buys or holds, the products' prices (wholesale and suggested retail), distributor turnover, and so on, are not part of the legal definition of a pyramid scheme and these, therefore, do not replace a compensation analysis in determining the legality of the firm's DS structure.

By contrast, a legitimate DS firm's compensation system does not offer compensation for recruitment without regard to sales. The rest of this chapter's discussion concerns such legitimate DS distributor compensation plans. A legitimate DS compensation plan can, however, offer commissions based on the sales of recruited downline distributors, whether

---

[9] As explained in the *Amway* case, recruitment-based compensation may be financially supported by high enrollment fees or inventory purchases incurred by new distributors: "168. Some multilevel direct selling companies have engaged in 'pyramid selling,' involving 'inventory loading' and 'headhunting' fees. These companies have a large inventory requirement for a new distributor, and reward distributors for bringing into the business a new distributor. The result emphasizes recruiting of new distributors rather than selling the products to consumers. Typically, these pyramid companies require new recruits to buy $2000 to $5000 in inventory, with as much as half of that amount going to the recruiting distributor" (Patty, Tr. 3091–3092). *In the Matter of Amway Corp.*, 93 F.T.C. 618, 1979 FTC LEXIS 390, *108 (F.T.C. 1979).

[10] See the discussions in Brockett, Coughlan, Ferrell, Ferrell, Golden, Ingene, Pelton, and Peterson (2020) and Coughlan (2020) for legal references that some argue support this point of view and a rebuttal of this argument.

these sales are to nondistributor end-users or are for voluntary personal consumption by the downline distributors.

The General Structure of a DS Firm's Distributor Compensation Plan

The DS firm's compensation plan encourages distributors of all types, and with varying goals and purposes, to sell the firm's products to nondistributors, to recruit and mentor downline distributors, and to enjoy the firm's products as personal consumers if they wish. This section discusses the structure and common elements in a DS distributor compensation plan and the logic for these elements. The next section shows how these elements work in an example reflecting common compensation practices in real DS firms.

The DS firm typically offers the same compensation plan to any and all distributors. This means that any distributor has access to the full compensation plan, and if she meets the criteria for a particular tier of compensation at a particular point in time, she is awarded that compensation. If she ceases to meet the performance requirements for that compensation level, her compensation adjusts to her new compensation tier. A logical consequence of this commonality of exposure to the full compensation plan is that the DS firm neither restricts the number of people who may achieve a particular level of compensation nor requires a distributor to "interview" to "qualify" at a particular earnings level. Her performance is the criterion for qualification. As a corollary, the number of distributors at any given earning level in the DS compensation plan may increase or decrease over time. In contrast, a firm running a non-DS employee sales force typically restricts the number of people in each tier of the sales force—for example, there is just one national sales manager per country and just one regional vice president of sales for each predefined geographic sales region.

Among all the types of joiners, a DS firm accepts registrants who join only because they like the firm's products and wish to consume them at a distributor discount price. Such participants can be called "intentional personal consumers" (IPCs) who do not aspire to build either a retail selling business or a downline network. Some DS firms allow these individuals to join a special "Preferred Customer" category, which gives them access to the distributor (or similar) product discounts but does not allow them to earn under the full compensation plan; other firms simply allow them to register as regular distributors and choose their method of participation. The IPC segment of distributors is sometimes incorrectly argued to have "lost money" from participating. However, the analysis in the next section shows that whether or not these individuals are categorized separately as Preferred Customers, they typically do not lose money from joining.

A second key feature of DS compensation plans is their lack of a salary component. This is sensible, given distributors' entrepreneurial, independent contractor status. Non-DS sales channels similarly do not offer salary to independent sales representatives, independent distributor firms, or franchisees, instead rewarding them through commissions, wholesale-to-retail markups, and residual profits.

The main compensation elements used in DS distributor compensation plans are of two types: wholesale-to-retail markups and commissions/bonuses based on a distributor's sales management skills (rewarding the ability to build and maintain a downline distributor network and the ability to train and motivate those downline distributors to generate retail sales and develop sales-productive downlines in their turn, respectively).

A wholesale-to-retail markup is simply the difference between the wholesale price paid for a unit of one of the DS firm's products and its suggested list (retail) price, which is set by the DS firm. The practice of offering wholesale price discounts to distributors is exactly the same as that used in non-DS channels with independent intermediaries such as distributors and retailers. In retailing, markups are generally calculated as a percentage of suggested retail price. For example, a wholesale price of US$12 per unit and a suggested retail price of US$20 per unit implies a retail markup percentage of 40 percent (US$8 divided by US$20). The dollar markup gives the distributor a reward for successfully exerting sales effort to sell at the suggested retail price. Because the DS distributor (like any non-DS retailer or distributor) is an independent contractor, she has the right to set any price for any unit she sells at retail, including prices lower than the suggested list levels. If she can make sales more easily (with less effort) by setting lower retail prices and therefore foregoing some retail markup, she is free to do so. The wholesale-to-retail markup is thus a key motivator of retail selling in the DS distributor force.

Other incentives are sometimes offered to encourage retail sales of particular products or product lines, just as occurs in non-DS retail channels. New products may offer a higher markup percentage during a "launch period," for example, or holiday incentives may encourage sales of items that can be given as gifts. Because these compensation elements do not account for a substantial portion of retail markup earnings in general, they are not further analyzed in this chapter.

Commissions and/or bonuses (sometimes also called "overrides" or "override commissions/bonuses") in DS distributor compensation plans reward a distributor's effort and success in building a downline of productive distributors—that is, they reward achievement as a sales manager. The typical plan includes criteria for each tier in the compensation plan (such as the maintenance of a certain level of one's own retail sales, the maintenance of a downline of a certain sales performance, and possibly size/structure) and always awards commission/bonus on the sales performance of that network. In other words, a bonus or commission may be predicated on the size and nature of the distributor's downline, but it is the achieved sales of those downline distributors that determine the bonus/commission award. For example, a given commission tier that requires this distributor to personally sell at least US$300 (wholesale value) of product per month and to have four downline distributors does *not* award the same compensation to all who are in that tier. Rather, their earned commission is a function of the sales of their downline.

It is common for the marginal commission/bonus rate to increase with the overall achievement of the distributor. Such a commission plan, called a "progressive commission" in non-DS sales organizations, is very common because of the strong incentive it gives the best sales managers to achieve at their highest potentials. It also reflects a standard principle of distribution channel implementation: that greater rewards must be offered for the achievement of higher levels of performance if the channel captain wishes to attract and retain the best sales managers in its force.

Finally, DS firms often offer a distinct reward to their very highest achievers, through a "Leadership Bonus Pool" or "President's Club" (or other similarly named compensation elements). Awards are earned for achievements such as cumulative group sales or the number and sales levels of other top-performing distributors they have mentored in their downlines over the bonus pool period.

In sum, the major ways in which the DS firm rewards its distributor force for performing the channel functions it has delegated to it include the following:

- Wholesale discounts on all units ordered (including units for personal consumption);
- Commissions and/or bonuses based on the sales of downline distributors recruited by the business-building distributor; and
- Leadership bonus pool for the very highest performers.

Specific Elements of a DS Compensation Plan and an Example

This section explains the specific financial elements and parameters of a DS reward and compensation plan that motivates distributors who join for various reasons, including IPCs, retail sellers, downline business builders, and those who value any combination of these three major reasons for participating. It shows how a typical multilevel DS distributor compensation plan leads to the various rewards. The plan depicted is a "nonbinary" plan, in contrast to alternative binary compensation plans in which a business-building distributor earns commissions based on building and motivating two (or more) "legs" of downline distributors. Because both types of plans share the key features of rewards for both retail sales and business-building success, we focus on the nonbinary plan in this chapter.

Financial Benefit of Voluntary Personal Consumption at Wholesale Prices

Many DS distributors join after discovering and enjoying the DS firm's products as a nondistributor retail consumer. This is a well-known phenomenon and personal consumption at wholesale rather than retail prices is a reasonable reward for a distributor's loyalty to this firm's products. These consumers can easily recognize that they benefit economically by paying an annual enrollment fee in return for being able to consume the products they love at wholesale prices. Individuals who join with this sole purpose are called "IPCs." Such a distributor[11] can accrue a net financial benefit from joining, even without engaging in retail selling or in developing a downline distributor network.

To illustrate with a specific example, her financial outlay as a nondistributor retail consumer of X units per year at the suggested retail price per unit of $\$P$ [12] is

Total costs of nondistributor retail consumption = $\$(P \times X)$

Meanwhile, her financial outlay as an "IPC" distributor for the same number of units, X, at wholesale price W per unit, and accounting for the DS firm's annual registration/renewal fee of $\$R$, is

Total costs of IPC distributor consumption = $\$(W \times X) + \$R$

Comparison of the two expressions shows the break-even point in terms of annual units of consumption, above which this IPC is better off enrolling as a distributor than remaining as a nondistributor retail consumer. That is, IPC is preferred to nondistributor status if

$$\$(W \times X) + \$R < \$(P \times X) \rightarrow X > R/(P - W)$$

In other words, a high enough voluntary personal consumption rate makes it economically and financially beneficial to join as a distributor, even if the distributor never earns any retail markup income or any commission check from the DS firm. The previous calculation shows that

---

[11] Or "Preferred Customer," if the DS firm has such a participant category.

[12] For simplicity, this analysis imagines sales of a single product that has a single suggested retail price of $P and wholesale price of $W, with W < P. This analysis is also applicable to the weighted average price savings in the case of a product line (with each product having its own {$W, $P} pair), rather than a single product.

the minimum necessary consumption level is greater, the higher is the annual registration/renewal fee of R. It is lower, the higher is the whole-sale-to-retail markup of $(P - W)$ dollars.[13]

It is important to note that this financial benefit of a distributorship is typically not recorded in the DS firm's compensation database. There-fore, it may seem that all distributors of this type lose money—at the rate of $R per year. However, in reality, such individuals do not lose money by enrolling as distributors precisely because they realize that they can breakeven on the annual registration/renewal fee when their desired con-sumption level is high enough. Such a threshold is often not hard to reach, since the annual registration/renewal fee for most DS firms is a reasonable amount of US$50 to US$100.

Markup Compensation for Retail Selling

Because the DS firm has spun off all responsibility for retail sales to its distributor force, the DS firm compensates its distributors for retail sell-ing success. Just as in non-DS distribution channels where, for instance, a manufacturer grants a wholesale discount to retailers selling its products, the DS firm quotes a wholesale price and a suggested retail (list) price for all of the products in its product line. The difference between suggested list price and wholesale price, $(P - W)$, is called the "retail markup" per product. Given distributors' status as independent contractors, each dis-tributor is free to set whatever retail price she wishes. Her retail markup income overall is the sum of all markups earned on all of her retail sales over a given period.

Suggested or list retail prices are often set at approximately twice the wholesale price level. This implies a retail margin of 50 percent on retail

---

[13] This calculation ignores the possibility of delivery charges to receive an order. A nondistributor retail consumer may not face any delivery charges if her dis-tributor delivers product to her or sells it to her in a party plan format. This indi-vidual may face delivery charges if she chooses to enroll as a distributor, however. If her yearly delivery costs amount to D, the break-even point above changes to: $X > (R+D)/(P - W)$, implying a higher amount of annual consumption for enrollment to be financially preferable to nondistributor retail consumption.

price (i.e., the retail markup equals one-half of the suggested list price). Such a markup structure is very common in non-DS retailing and is known as *keystone pricing*.

Whatever the size of the targeted retail margin set by the DS firm, it denotes a budgeted allocation of a portion of total channel revenues to the distributor force. For example, a DS or non-DS firm practicing keystone pricing budgets half of the total channel's revenues for distributors' earnings from retail selling. This significant proportion of the total channel's revenue potential is consistent with the crucial role played by the distributor force as the only channel member category engaged in retail sales generation.

Despite the high proportion of total channel revenues budgeted for distributors' retail markup income, most DS firms do not have a reliable or automated means of measuring each distributor's retail sales income. Just as in non-DS distribution channels using independent distributors or retailers, the DS distributor's independent contractor status means that she is the master of her own business decisions, including how to set retail prices and what to sell. Because of this, it is typically not possible to report retail markup income as part of the entire compensation system the DS firm offers. Like the financial benefit from voluntary personal consumption, this may lead some to ignore retail income in calculating the overall economic and financial benefit of a distributorship and therefore to conclude erroneously that all nonbusiness-building distributors "lose money" in their distributorships. Despite this, many DS distributors who are not interested in recruiting other distributors or acting as "sales managers" have thriving retail businesses and renew their DS distributorships year after year to continue enjoying these benefits.

This can be seen in an extension of our earlier example. Consider the following:

- The distributor does not personally consume any units of product.[14]

---

[14] This assumption is for clarity only. It allows us to see the financial returns to retail selling specifically. The distributor who both personally consumes and sells at retail makes a higher financial return than that calculated here.

- She does not have a downline and thus does not earn commissions from the firm.
- She buys inventory of the firm's product (assumed for simplicity to be a single product) at wholesale price $\$W$ per unit.
- She orders X units of product per month.
- She incurs a delivery cost of $\$D$ per delivery, for a yearly delivery cost of $\$(12 \times D)$.
- She sells her inventory[15] at an average retail price of $\$P$ per unit (which may be the DS firm's suggested list price or some other price).[16]
- She pays an annual registration/renewal fee of $\$R$.

Then this distributor's net earnings after all costs for the year are made up of

$$\text{Net Revenue per Month} = \$[(P - W) \times X]$$
$$\text{Incurred Delivery Costs} = \$(12 \times D)$$
$$\text{Incurred Annual Registration/Renewal Fee} = \$R$$

These imply that it is financially profitable to join purely as a retail seller when

$$\$[12 \times (P - W) \times X - 12 \times D - R] > 0$$

---

[15] This assumes that the distributor does not overorder inventory (thus avoiding an ongoing inventory holding cost). DS firms typically warn distributors against inventory-loading and encourage them to match their ordering practices to their selling abilities. Yet other DS firms avert inventory costs by offering drop-shipping directly to her nondistributor end-users.

[16] Note that this omits any costs of spending time selling. Since such factors vary widely across any DS firm's distributor force, they cannot be predicted by the DS firm at the individual–distributor level. For example, a distributor who either has no other job or engages in the DS selling opportunity only in her free time is not said to have a high opportunity cost of time; that is, the retail DS income earned may be entirely incremental to any other personal or household income potential.

Retail selling alone is thus profitable, for example, when the achievable retail markup is high enough relative to delivery and registration/renewal fees—and the necessary markup for profitability is lower, the higher is the distributor's unit sales volume, as shown in the following equation:

$$(P - W) > (D/X) + R/(12 \times X)$$

Furthermore, the distributor makes a net profit at a lower retail markup and/or a lower sales rate, the higher is her voluntary personal consumption, since that consumption generates a compensating financial benefit of its own.

Therefore, a distributor who never earns a commission check from the DS firm, but who successfully engages in retail selling (and possibly voluntary personal consumption), can profit from the DS opportunity even if her success is not routinely trackable by the DS firm. Erroneously inferring that such distributors have "lost money" ignores these rewards, which are a direct function of the DS firm's budgeting for retail markup income through its wholesale and suggested retail price lists. These markups are an important part of the DS firm's overall compensation structure because of their key motivating effect on retail sales effort by the distributor force.

Commission Compensation for Building and Maintaining a Productive Distributor Downline

Beyond the financial benefits of voluntary personal consumption at wholesale prices and of retail markup income, the DS firm also compensates those distributors who recruit and mentor other distributors who produce retail sales (whether through voluntary personal consumption and/or nondistributor sales). This set of recruits is called the distributor's "downline." The downline consists of those individuals directly recruited by this distributor—called "frontline distributors"—and all others recruited downline from them.

Recruiting and mentoring a productive downline is not a trivial task. Not only is being a business-builder time-consuming, but success at these functions requires sales, marketing, and management skills. Some distributors lack the requisite skills and time, making successful and motivated business builders a valuable and nonubiquitous part of the distributor force. Were the DS firm not to reward successful business-building efforts, distributors would not invest the ongoing time and effort to build a network. Since the DS firm's distribution channel strategy involves allocating all recruiting and sales management efforts to the distributor force, an appropriate reward system is therefore crucial to the DS firm's success.

Compensation for these recruiting and management activities is typically awarded through a sales-based commission structure, often quoted as a percentage of wholesale dollar sales or a points-based function of wholesale dollar sales.[17] Because many or most DS firms cannot observe actual personal consumption and actual retail sales of each distributor because of their independent contractor status,[18] the standard practice has been to offer commissions on distributors' *purchases* of product from the DS firm, rather than on the ultimate *sales* of those units of product. This raises the possibility that an unscrupulous upline distributor might urge her downlines to overorder inventory (i.e., to *inventory-load*) without a realistic expectation that this higher level of inventory matches the downline's expected sales ability. The upline would benefit from this because her total group volume would increase, thus increasing the commission rate for which she would qualify.

DS firms have long used various "protections" to mitigate the possibility of inventory loading in pursuit of higher commissions. Some of the most common of these are given as follows[19]:

- A requirement that at least 70 percent of the prior volume ordered has been sold before placing a new order;

---

[17] These are sometimes called "bonuses," "overrides," "override commissions," or other similar words. This discussion will use the term "commission" for simplicity, and later uses "bonus" for distinct higher level rewards.

[18] See Chapter 4 for a discussion of technological advances in DS monitoring and enforcement of product and earnings claims. Some companies have innovated retail sales-tracking technologies used to link commissions more directly to retail sales, but perfect measurement of retail sales is still not possible at most DS companies.

[19] For a more in-depth discussion of the protections, see Coughlan (2019).

- A requirement to keep evidence of having sold to at least some fixed number of retail consumers per month (e.g., 10);
- A requirement to offer each retail buyer a receipt showing the items sold at prices paid and to stand ready to show these receipts to the firm whenever asked; and
- An offer by the firm to departing distributors to buy back their resellable inventory at 90 percent or more of the original wholesale purchase price, in order to take excess inventory off the resigning distributor's hands. Along with this repurchase provision, the firm then claws back any commissions earned on these purchased (but not sold) units by an upline distributor, thus mitigating the original financial incentives to urge inventory on downlines.

Under these protections, commissions offered on purchases, when retail sales are not observable, are a good method of preserving the incentive to engage in retail selling and network-building activities while protecting against opportunistic distributor behavior. This chapter's discussion will thus use the term "sales" with the understanding that purchases may be the measurable proxy for sales on which commissions are awarded. Some terminology will aid in explaining the DS distributor commission plan. For simplicity, the discussion assumes that any "points" system allocates one point to each dollar of wholesale sales.

Commissions are usually awarded based on "group volume," which includes all downline sales and the distributor's direct retail sales, typically including voluntary personal consumption by the distributor herself.[20] The specifics are best explained with an example. This example assumes that sales are accounted for, and commissions are paid, monthly.

---

[20] Whether or not personal consumption is considered part of the distributor's "group volume" does not affect the general structure or motivational power of the compensation plan. For example, instead of including personal consumption in group volume—perhaps as a means of rewarding brand loyalty—the firm could instead commensurately increase the wholesale discount on distributor purchases.

Consider one distributor, "Anne," and her downline distributor network. Anne's "personal volume," or PV, is defined as the sum of Anne's personal product consumption and Anne's retail sales to her own nondistributor consumers in wholesale dollars. Anne's "group volume," or GV, is defined as the sum of Anne's PV and the PVs of each of Anne's downline distributors.

Then Anne qualifies for a higher commission rate, the greater is her GV. Such a schedule rewards her both for her own selling ability and for the ability to find, mentor, and develop a sales-productive downline. Specifically, Table 3.2 reports the commission rate that Anne can qualify for based on her GV in this month.

Table 3.2 Monthly commission rate qualification as a percent of group volume (GV)

Monthly commission rate qualified for (as % of GV):	
If monthly GV (in US$ wholesale sales) of:	Commission rate (%) on GV qualified for is:
$0–$99	0
$100–$250	2
$251–$500	4
$501–$1,000	6
$1,001–$2,000	9
$2,001–$4,000	13
$4,001–$8,000	18
$8,001 or higher	24

The PV and GV achieved this month by Anne and each of the distributors in her downline can be seen by looking at her downline network's performance, as shown in Figure 3.1. Anne has three frontline distributors: Betty, Claire, and Diane. Betty has recruited one downline, Elaine, who has recruited Frances. Claire has no downline. Diane has recruited Ginny, who has recruited Helen, who has recruited Isabelle.

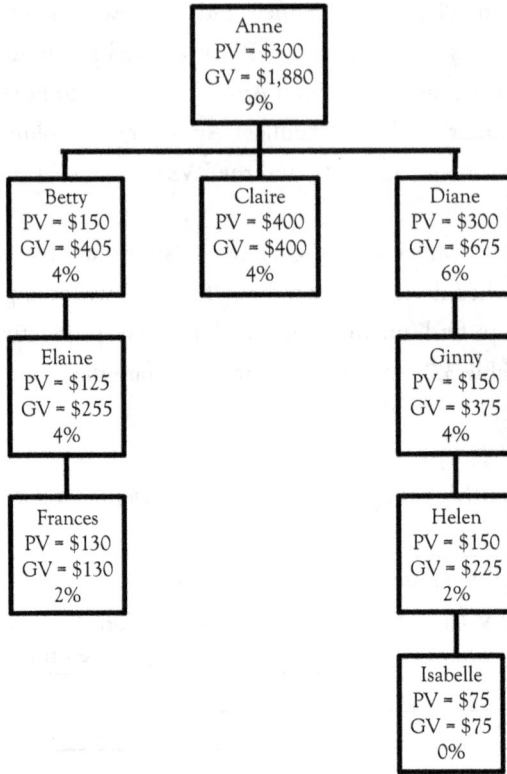

Figure 3.1 Anne's network's PVs, GVs, and qualified commission rates (USD)

Anne thus has eight distributors in her downline, with varying numbers of downlines themselves. Each person's PV equals the wholesale dollar value of her own personal consumption plus direct sales to nondistributor consumers. Each person's GV equals the sum of her own PV plus the PVs of each of her downline distributors (or equivalently, plus the GV of her frontline). Thus, Elaine's PV is US$125, but her GV is US$255, reflecting both her PV and that of her single downline, Frances.

The graphic also notes the commission rate each distributor qualifies for this month, matching that person's GV to the qualification commission rates in Table 3.2. Isabelle's GV of US$75 does not qualify her for any commission (although she may have made retail markup income beyond the commission compensation structure). Frances and Helen each qualify for a 2 percent commission; Betty, Elaine, Claire, and Ginny qualify for a 4 percent commission; Diane qualifies for a 6 percent commission; and Anne qualifies for a 9 percent commission.

Given that the commission rate is a function of a person's GV, one might be tempted to think that multiple distributors could earn the commission on a given unit sale. However, this is not so. An upline earns the full commission qualified for on the value of her own PV; but she earns only an *override* percentage on the GVs of her downlines, where the override is the difference between the upline's qualified commission rate and the downline's qualified commission rate. For example, Elaine (qualifying for a 4 percent commission) earns that full 4 percent on her own PV but earns only (4 percent to 2 percent), or 2 percent, on Frances' sales. This commission system thus simultaneously motivates direct sales (through Elaine's commissions on her own PV) and successful sales management

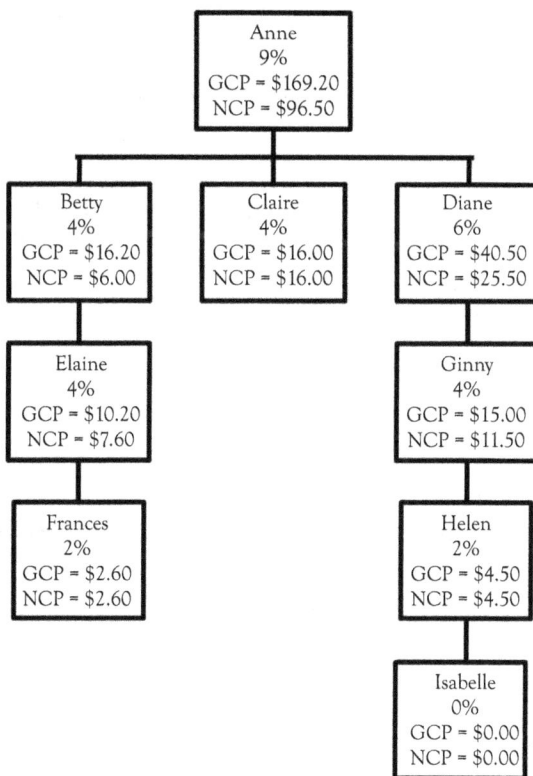

Figure 3.2 Anne's network's qualified commission rates, gross (GCP) and net commission payments (NCP) (USD)

(through Elaine's override commissions on Frances' sales). Extended across the full commission and network structure, this provision prevents double or more commission payments on the same unit sale and implies a predictable budget for the DS firm's total compensation costs.

This example shows that a distributor's commission status is not a strict function of her position in the DS firm's distributor network, but rather a function of her personal sales performance and that of her downline. To see this, consider Betty. She has a slightly higher PV than either of her downlines, Elaine and Frances. While her GV (US$405) is larger than Elaine's (US$255), both qualify for a 4 percent commission. Thus, the typical DS distributor commission plan does not award a distributor's mere position in the network; instead, all awards are identifiably sales-based.

Now we know each distributor's personal and downline group performance this month. In a real DS firm, these data are collected continuously and stored in a database sometimes called the "LOS" (Line of Sponsorship). Then, how much commission does each distributor in this structure earn?

Recalling the override concept described previously, Figure 3.2 lists again each distributor's qualified commission rate and uses the other information from Figure 3.1 to calculate the "Gross Commission Payment" (GCP) and the "Net Commission Payment" (NCP) for distributors Anne through Isabelle. GCP is defined as the total amount of commission payments to a distributor's group, which includes the distributor herself and her downline distributors (e.g., Elaine's group includes Elaine and Frances). NCP is defined as the commission earned by this distributor herself, which equals her GCP minus the GCP of each of her frontline distributors (e.g., Elaine's NCP equals Elaine's GCP minus Frances' GCP). Specifically, Elaine's NCP equals her GCP (US$10.20) minus her downlines' GCPs— here, Elaine's GCP (US$2.60). Elaine's NCP is therefore US$7.60. All other GCPs and NCPs are reported and calculated analogously.

Note that consistent with Figure 3.1's reporting of a zero-commission rate for Isabelle, Figure 3.2 reports that indeed, Isabelle earned zero commissions this month—both because her PV is too low to merit commission and because she has no downline.

Table 3.3 Net commission payments (NCP) this month

Distributor	NCP this month in US$
Anne	87.50
Betty	6.00
Claire	16.00
Diane	25.50
Elaine	7.60
Frances	2.60
Ginny	10.50
Helen	4.50
Isabelle	0.00
Total commission payments to Anne and her downline this month	160.20

Also of note is the fact that generally—but not necessarily—one's NCP is higher, the larger is one's downline. Exceptions to this generally believable pattern are instructive. For example, Claire earns a higher commission check this month (US$16.00) than does Betty, despite the fact that their GVs are almost identical (US$400 and US$405, from Figure 3.1) and Betty's downline is larger than Claire's. The reasons that Claire nevertheless earns a larger commission check are first that she is a stronger retail seller than Betty, with a PV of US$400 versus Betty's US$150. The second reason is that while Betty "catches up" to Claire in GV, she does so with a downline (Elaine) who has achieved the same 4 percent commission rate as Betty. Therefore, while Betty does gain the benefit of a higher qualified commission rate than she would have enjoyed with only her own PV, she earns commission only on her own PV, which is lower than Claire's. Furthermore, note that Betty earns a lower commission check this month than does her own frontline, Elaine: Betty's NCP is just US$6.00, while Elaine's is US$7.60.

These combined insights reinforce the fact that a well-designed and legitimate DS distributor compensation plan does not award compensation for mere recruitment of a downline. It is the combination of all members' sales that creates commissionable income. This implies that rank or position in the DS firm's distributor network is no guarantee of the income one can earn relative to those at an apparently "lower" position in the network. Such insights are characteristic of the plan of a legitimate DS firm rather than of an illegal pyramid scheme.

In summary, the commission checks paid to each of these distributors this month are as shown in Table 3.3.

It is useful to consider the compensation plan not only from the point of view of each *distributor* but also from the point of view of a *particular product unit sold*. Consider a unit that Isabelle sells. She earns *no* commission on this unit (although she likely earns retail markup income on it). Her volume rolls up to her immediate upline, Helen, who earns 2 percent on that unit. Helen's upline, Ginny, earns 2 percent on this unit as well, which is Ginny's override (her 4 percent qualification rate minus Helen's 2 percent rate). Diane, Ginny's upline, earns an override of 2 percent on this unit as well (equal to Diane's 6 percent qualification rate minus Ginny's 4 percent qualification rate). Finally, Diane's upline Anne earns an override of 3 percent on this unit (equal to Anne's 9 percent qualification rate minus Diane's 6 percent qualification rate). This unit, therefore, costs the firm 9 percent in commissions in this example. If we were to map a larger portion of this firm's entire distributor network, we would likely discover total commission payouts of 24 percent for this unit, due to the overall structure of the commission plan as noted in Table 3.2. However, given Table 3.2 and the nature of override payments, the DS firm can budget for commission expenses at a maximum of 24 percent of its wholesale sales.

Higher Level Bonus Compensation Elements

Other parts of a DS firm's compensation structure, also all sales-based, reward higher levels of performance and achievement. This chapter will not develop all such elements in detail, but the main insights can be seen from understanding two such rewards: *breakaway bonuses* and *leadership bonus pools*.

Breakaway bonus. The fundamental reason to offer any compensation is to provide an incentive for distributors to perform the desired channel functions allocated to them and, as a correlate, to reduce any *disincentive* to do so. One such disincentive can arise when an upline distributor recruits a downline who becomes in her turn a very productive retail seller and downline network builder. For clarity, let us call the original upline distributor "A" and her very productive downline "B."

DS firms typically establish a criterion for this "very productive" level of behavior by downline B. It can include B's retail selling prowess, the number and productivity of B's downline distributors, the number of B's downline distributors who themselves build sales-productive downlines, strings of months of high performance per year, and so on. Once B has reached such a threshold, the DS firm designates B and her downlines as a "breakaway" from A's commissionable network of downlines. The logic for separating B from A's downline is that B's high achievement level indicates that mentoring and guidance from A is no longer a driving influence on the sales performance in B's downline. Returning to the basic reason for offering compensation, we recognize that A no longer is "doing the work" or "generating the value" and therefore should not continue to draw override commissions based on B's group performance.

While this is very logical, designating B's downline as a breakaway can have a very significant negative effect on A's commission qualification level and amount of total commission income. To ease the financial pain this can cause and to preserve A's incentive to mentor highly productive downline distributors, DS firms typically offer a different type of income to A that is predicated on her very significant achievement of having mentored a leader in her own right. This reward usually is called a "bonus" to distinguish it from the commission structure. Often, the breakaway bonus is a fixed percentage (such as 1 percent) of the wholesale sales in B's breakaway group. If multiple downlines of A become breakaways in their own right (say, also group C and group D, for three total breakaway groups under A), the breakaway bonus often increases, for example to 2 percent of the wholesale value of sales in each of these groups.

Leadership bonus pool. If A is highly productive, both in maintaining her own active downline network and in recruiting and mentoring multiple downlines to breakaway, the DS firm can also award "bonus points" for each significant business building and breakaway achievement over a period of one year.[21] The firm precommits to a certain bonus pool formula or amount that will be split among all qualifiers proportionately to their amassed points over the year. Often the bonus pool is set at a prespecified percentage of the entire DS firm's wholesale sales for the year (e.g., 2 percent of the firm's wholesale sales). Suppose then at the end of the year that 150 distributors have earned at least one point; that 500 points in total have been earned by these 150 distributors; and that the firm's wholesale sales have been US$600 million this year. Then the leadership bonus pool is funded this year at US$12 million (US$600 million times 0.02), and each point is therefore worth US$24,000 (US$12 million divided by 500). A distributor who has earned three points is therefore paid US$72,000 in leadership bonus, and one who has earned one point is paid US$24,000.

Note that like all other compensation elements, the Leadership Bonus Pool is based on productivity driven by sales. A point earned by an upline who has mentored a breakaway would seem to be a recruitment-driven reward, but in fact no reward at all would be earned but for the fact that a breakaway is defined by a certain overall sales performance level.

Comments on, and Summary of, DS Distributor Compensation Plans

Some important highlights of the previous discussion of DS distributor compensation include the following:

- The DS compensation plan is offered in full and equally to all distributors.
- DS compensation plans include elements that reward *consumption loyalty* (through wholesale discounts on voluntary personal consumption of the firm's products), *retailing to non-distributor consumers* (through retail markups often set at 50 percent of suggested list prices), and *recruiting and mentoring*

---

[21] The bonus pool could span a shorter time period as well, of course. A year is, however, the most common period for amassing qualification for a Leadership Bonus Pool award.

other sales-productive distributors (through commissions and higher level performance awards).

- Even though compensation can be earned by virtue of a network of productive distributors several levels down from the upline distributor, no "infinite commissions" are offered, because on any *given unit sold*, a *fixed and calculable amount is paid out in commissions throughout the distributor network.*
- The DS firm's compensation structure thus mathematically guarantees a maximum distributor compensation budget to the firm … so the existence of multilevel compensation is not an automatic sign that the firm is operating a pyramid scheme that is doomed to fail.
- DS distributor compensation rewards thus provide incentives for both "field sales" and "sales manager" level achievements. Even voluntary personal consumers are rewarded for their product loyalty via financial savings from personal consumption at wholesale rather than retail prices.

How Legitimate DS Compensation Is Typically Distributed Across the Distributor Force as a Result

This chapter has focused on the nature and structure of the DS distributor compensation plan itself. It is worthwhile to discuss what this structure implies for the overall distribution of compensation across the distributor force as a result. Three major implications are discussed here, of particular interest because they may erroneously indicate to the naïve observer that the DS firm is operating an illegal pyramid scheme and/or is misleading distributor prospects about the DS business opportunity.

A Majority of Distributors May Earn No Commissions or Bonuses

DS firms' Income Disclosure Statements frequently show that most distributors earn no commissions or bonuses from the firm. Sometimes such evidence fuels an argument that the firm operates a pyramid scheme and/or that the firm fraudulently misrepresents the business opportunity offered to distributors.

However, this argument is unfounded, first because many join for reasons other than to make commission or bonus income. These may include joining for personal consumption at wholesale rather than retail prices or for the social interaction inherent in the DS distribution channel form and person-to-person selling mode. The absence of commission or bonus payments to such participants is not a signal of either pyramid scheme operation or misrepresentation of the business opportunity, and these participants cannot be said to have lost money through participating. On the contrary, as independent contractors, these participants choose not to exert effort or invest in skills to improve their retail selling or business-building abilities.

Second, many distributors join and successfully engage in retail selling as well. Because most DS firms cannot reliably track retail sales or voluntary personal consumption, they cannot document the amount of earned retail markup income or the financial benefit of personal consumption at wholesale price reductions. Income Disclosure Statements therefore significantly underreport actual earned income. As an illustration, consider the fact that the typical retail markup on a DS firm's product line of 50 percent of the list price of the products is equal to one-half of the total channel's revenue potential or, equivalently, is equal to the entire wholesale revenue of the DS firm. Meanwhile, the DS firm's budget for commission and bonus payments is often just 10 percent to 15 percent of the DS firm's wholesale revenues. This means that the observable income paid out by the firm (commissions and bonuses) may be only about one-tenth of the retail markup potential! Even if distributors sometimes offer products for a discount off list price, these margins still allow retail profits to be made. One, therefore, cannot conclude that many "lose money" by participating when one observes that most distributors do not earn a commission or bonus check over an entire year.

The Average Annual Commission and Bonus Payout to Those Distributors Who Do Earn One or More Payments Is Often Very Low per Distributor

Income Disclosure Statements frequently report on the earnings of those distributors who earn at least one commission or bonus payment from the firm over the year. Median, average, and sometimes the 25th and 75th percentiles of earnings are reported. Despite separating out the population of distributors who earned no commission or bonus, the statistics often still show low annual earnings, often much below any full-time income level. This observation, like the first one, sometimes triggers a conclusion that the business opportunity is chimerical or that the firm is likely to collapse.

However, this, too, is a naïve conclusion that fails to take account of the inherent nature of the independent contractor character of DS. In particular, each distributor chooses her own work hours and extent of work each week and month throughout the year; the DS firm does not measure hours of work or urge/require any minimum amount of effort. Seasonal, not year-round, work is also allowed, which may help the distributor pay for particular expenses (such as the cost of summer camp for the children) but is unlikely to facilitate the building of a productive downline or the earning of commissions from the firm.

Furthermore, because enrollment as a distributor is easy, generally low cost, and open to virtually everyone, sales and sales management skills in the distributor force exhibit high variance. Many may enroll without any prior sales experience at all, while some may enroll who have participated in other DS firms. The DS firm, therefore, does not screen on enrollees with high potential to sell at retail or build a large downline. All are given the opportunity to do so, through the common offering of the full compensation plan to all, but the combination of varying underlying skill levels and the right to choose low work hours explains low average or median income earnings across the distributor force.

Thus, low average or median earnings have many plausible explanations that have nothing to do with the operation of a fraudulent business opportunity or a pyramid scheme.

A Small Proportion of Distributors Often Earns a Large Proportion of Total Commission and Bonus Payments

Connected with the prior two points, it is common to observe a (sometimes very) small proportion of distributors making a (sometimes very) large proportion of all commission and bonus payments awarded by the DS firm. Some appeal to this observation to support a pyramid scheme allegation by arguing that only a few, or only the early joiners, can possibly make large incomes in this business. Nevertheless, as with the previous observations, this too is insufficient to prove that a pyramid scheme is in play.

One reason is that the skill set to build and run a large, vibrant, and sales-productive downline as an entrepreneurial distributor is not a common or basic talent set in the population at large. In non-DS sales forces, by analogy, it is often observed that a good sales manager is a rare person and cannot be predicted even when choosing from among the best field salespeople the firm employs. Given this, it should not be surprising that those who do already have, or invest in training to acquire, selling and sales management skills, will tend to be those who accrue the highest commission and bonus earnings.

Another reason for concentration of DS income is that running a successful downline is generally considerably more time-consuming than retailing, which itself is more time-consuming than being an IPC. Since many enroll as DS distributors while maintaining their regular full-time job, the time available to build a strong network is not initially available and may never be available. The distributor's choice about how much time to spend on working her business, as well as on developing her retailing and management skills, is her own, not the firm's. This is likely to contribute to the overall income distribution in a DS firm's distributor force.

Conclusion

This chapter has established the role of compensation as a crucial motivator to one's distribution channel partners to perform the important functions delegated to them in the DS distribution channel. Without rewards for brand loyalty, sales generation, and sales management development and expertise, no firm could expect its sales force of nonemployee independent contractors to provide, altruistically, these inputs to a successful firm. Thus, DS distributor compensation must provide various incentives for these various functions to be done, all while allowing the freedom and openness characteristic of DS distributor enrollment and participation.

The discussion shows that the firm's commission and bonus system is not the only element of compensation. Personal consumption wholesale discounts to drive brand loyalty, markups from wholesale to retail prices to drive retailing effort, and commissions and bonuses to reward successful recruiting and mentoring of sales-productive downlines are all part of the DS firm's sharing of total channel revenues with its crucial distributor partners.

In addition to developing insight about how compensation works, the chapter also explains the multiple ways in which distributors can participate and earn real economic and financial benefits. Some of these, such as commissions and bonuses, are measured, tracked, and reported by the DS firm in its Income Disclosure Statements. Others, such as personal consumption financial benefits and unmeasured retail profits, are not.

Thus, the chapter also establishes that it is naïve to conclude that the firm operates an illegal pyramid scheme or is misleading prospects and distributors from observations like those about the proportion of participants who earn a commission or bonus or those about the distribution of measured income across the distributor population. Instead, a more careful analysis is indicated to establish the structure of the DS distribution channel and the key roles played by its compensation program.

References

Brockett, P.L., A.T. Coughlan, L. Ferrell, O.C. Ferrell, L.L. Golden, C. Ingene, L.E. Pelton, and R.A. Peterson. 2020. "Direct Selling Under Scrutiny: Assessing Analytic Direct Selling Models." SSRN Working Paper, http://dx.doi.org/10.2139/ssrn.3743816 (accessed February 25, 2021).

Coughlan, A.T. 2019. "Consumer Harm from Voluntary Business Arrangements: What Conditions are Necessary?" SSRN Working Paper, http://dx.doi.org/10.2139/ssrn.3488105, (accessed February 25, 2021).

Coughlan, A.T. 2020. "An Analysis of 'Marketing Fraud: An Approach for Differentiating Multilevel Marketing from Pyramid Schemes' Under Standard Protections Offered by Legitimate Direct Selling Firms." SSRN Working Paper, http://dx.doi.org/10.2139/ssrn.3718842 (accessed February 25, 2021).

In the Matter of Amway Corp., 93 F.T.C. 618, 1979 FTC LEXIS 390, *97 (F.T.C. 1979).

In the Matter of Koscot Interplanetary, Inc., 86 F.T.C. 1106, 1975 WL 173318, (F.T.C. 1975).

CHAPTER 4

Ethics and Compliance in Direct Selling

Linda K. Ferrell and O.C. Ferrell

As described in Chapter 2, the integrity of direct selling has been well-established, dating back to the earliest forms of direct-to-consumer marketing exchanges. Currently, this business model in the United States has the oversight of the Direct Selling Association (DSA) with formalized compliance requirements and a code of ethics, and the business model has ongoing monitoring by the Better Business Bureau (BBB) National Programs and the Federal Trade Commission (FTC). In this chapter, we examine how ethics and compliance are managed in the direct selling marketplace. First, we examine ethical issues in direct selling. Next, we look at the role of ethics and compliance programs in direct selling firms. Then, we look at the self-regulation within the direct selling marketplace, including how the DSA has partnered with the BBB National Programs for compliance monitoring of all direct selling firms.

Ethical Issues in Direct Selling

Despite direct selling being a long-established legitimate business model, it has become the target of biased misinterpretation in the mass media (Vesoulis and Dockterman 2020). Much of this misrepresentation relates to what is referred to as the faulty generalization fallacy. Fallacies are arguments based on defective logic, and the strawman fallacy is when the argument is oversimplified to make an easier attack. That is, the argument is based on a very weak accusation that excludes important information reflecting reality. With regard to direct selling, a few inferences about ethical misconduct have been generalized across the entire direct selling marketplace. Two of the most important issues facing direct selling companies are product claims and earnings claims.

Product Claims

There are two types of product claims. Express claims are actual statements that can be verified. Implied claims relate to the impression gained through words, phrases, and images. In other words, the claim may be true but convey an impression that is false and misleading. For example, the FTC found that "Don't wait until the next virus. PREVENT, PROTECT, AND MAINTAIN YOUR HEALTH. Boost your immune system now" implied that the nutritional supplement referenced would protect against or prevent COVID-19. Weight loss products also often have implied claims. That is, a testimonial that an individual lost 50 pounds in three months implies that the average user can expect to lose that same amount.

Puffery is accepted behavior because it is vague and no reasonable person would believe it or take the claim seriously, as it cannot be proven objectively. An example would be a laundry detergent that stated the outcome was to produce clothing that is "whiter than white." Whereas, to say that a laundry detergent reduces bacteria or creates a fresh scent is something that could be objectively challenged by a competitor and validated. Therefore, claims of all types must be truthful, accurate, and not misleading to cause a consumer to purchase a product based on "false information."

Substantiation will be required depending on the nature of the product and regulatory guidelines. The FTC more closely regulates health and nutrition claims than tangible products where the consumer can more readily judge attributes and performance. In direct selling, health and wellness products, including cosmetics and nutritional supplements, are scrutinized more often than household cleaning products, home décor, and cookware.

Earnings Claims

Earnings claims relate to providing income estimates to independent contractors who sell products for direct selling firms. The Direct Selling

Self-Regulatory Council (DSSRC) and the DSA provide guidance on acceptable earnings claims. Earnings claims are important because when the FTC investigates a direct selling company, exaggerated earnings provide a signal of misconduct and possible evidence to support the accusation of a pyramid scheme (which was described in Chapter 3).

The DSSRC defines earnings as any expressed or implied claim that conveys any of the following:

- A level or range of actual potential earnings.
- A level or range of gross or net income, including the ability to make lifestyle purchases (e.g., homes, vehicles, vacations, etc.).
- Any statement, representation, or scenario to suggest a direct seller can reasonably achieve a level of income.
- Any graphics, such as tables or calculations, demonstrating possible income.
- Marketing materials describing promising potential income amounts or extraordinary or lavish lifestyles.
- That company-sponsored incentives, including lifestyles, vacations, or rewards may be earned as a direct seller.

Firms must have accurate substantiations about expressed or implied income claims. The disclosures are necessary to ensure claims are truthful and not misleading. For example, disclosing median rather than average earnings separates the lower half from the upper half and provides more typical earnings than averaging the sales.

Testimonials are of concern because a claim that a salesperson made, for example, US$600 the first month implies new distributors can make this much in one month. To substantiate this claim would require: (a) the person did make US$600 the first month and (b) other salespersons typically make US$600 the first month. Claims such as "Have you been wanting a new Mercedes Benz or Porsche?", "Have you been wanting a new home?", or "Contact me to learn how you can achieve your wildest dreams" imply that anyone joining as a distributor can purchase luxury goods and a home. This is not puffery because the new recruits would possibly believe that the results are typical, and it could influence their decision to join the direct selling company as an independent distributor.

A reasonable person with limited business experience could believe this misrepresentation.

Many people who have no business experience are vulnerable to these types of claims. Images, such as those reflecting an exotic lifestyle through visuals of yachts, automobiles, private jets, or expensive vacations, used on social media in recruiting new distributors provide an implied representation that the recruit will have an earnings level to support that type of lifestyle. The DSSRC provides guidelines as to how to address earnings claims to avoid any legal or regulatory concerns.

The Role of Ethics and Compliance Programs

The ethics and compliance programs of direct selling companies are important in helping the companies avoid misconduct and legal/regulatory investigations. The direct selling marketplace faces challenges based on the business model of using independent contractors to sell company products. Since independent contractors are not employees, there are fewer opportunities to observe and monitor their activities. In addition, most direct selling firms have limited background checks. Many incoming distributors have limited/no business experience or knowledge of how to sell. Many people who join direct selling firms like the products and want to share these products with their friends and family. Some who want to have the business opportunity have no experience in operating a small business, few time management skills, limited communications skills, and/or lack the ability to market and digitally message in support of the business. This means the ethics and compliance responsibility for direct selling firms is enormous.

There needs to be extensive training, monitoring, and enforcement of the activities of distributors. The direct selling company needs to have an ethical organizational culture to establish shared values and compliance policies. Values are important to establish a core set of ideals and principles such as accountability, trust, respect, and integrity to guide the ethical decisions of company employees who are responsible for providing training and monitoring of independent contractors. Compliance creates control by requiring both employees of the company and independent contractors to commit to specific, required conduct. Compliance is related to legal requirements and policies to prevent potential misconduct that could damage a firm financially as well as its reputation.

The DSA Code of Ethics is important in guiding company codes of ethics and compliance policies. DSA members are required to abide by the code. The DSA has structured the code to provide policies that member companies agree to follow as a condition of membership. The Applicant and Member Company Review Process is robust, only allowing less than 50 percent of applicant companies to be accepted into membership. In addition, DSA selects 20 percent of member companies each year for an ethics and compliance review. Membership is discontinued for any companies that do not pass the review. Areas reviewed by DSA staff and attorneys include websites, compensation plans, product lines, marketing plans, product and income opportunities, and legal and regulatory records (see Figure 4.1).

Developing and implementing a code of ethics is important, but a comprehensive ethics and compliance program is needed for company

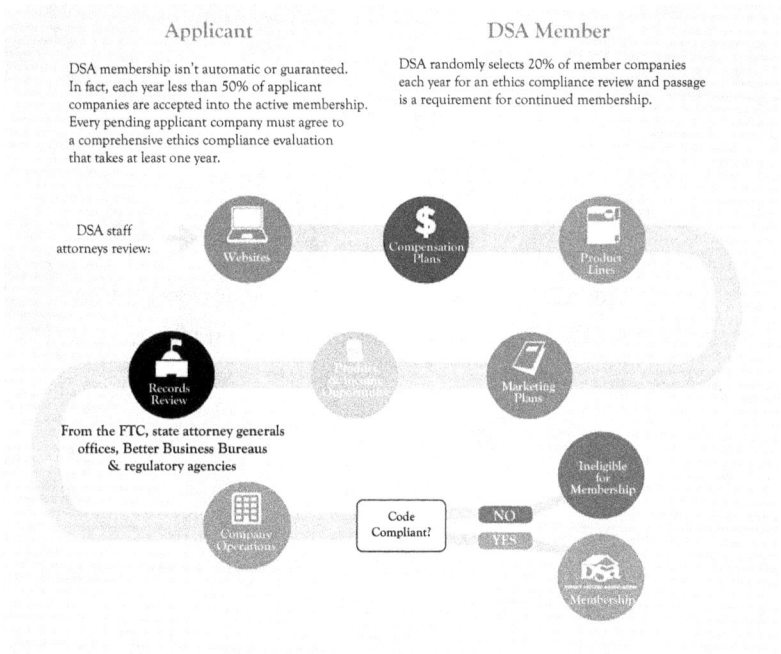

Figure 4.1 DSA code review process

Source: Direct Selling Association (2021a). Used with permission.

implementation. A comprehensive ethics and compliance program requires a variety of components. At a minimum, the following components of an ethics and compliance program should be required: ethics and compliance officers, training programs, monitoring systems, and continuous improvement efforts.

Ethics and Compliance Officers

The board of directors should provide oversight on the direct selling company's ethics and compliance program. Every company should have an ethics and compliance officer to oversee ethical and legal standards, and best practice is for the ethics and compliance officer to report directly to the board of directors. Areas of responsibility for the ethics and compliance officer include:

- Assessing risks that the program needs to address;
- The code of ethics and compliance requirement;
- Training of corporate employees as well as communication with independent contractors distributing the product;
- An open communications system to handle questions and complaints;
- Understanding and compliance with all governmental laws;
- Monitoring and auditing the activities of employees in the company as well as independent contractors;
- Taking action on any legal or ethical violations discovered; and
- Reviewing the effectiveness of the program and taking corrective action as needed or anticipated.

Training

Direct selling companies should require salesforce members who are actively pursuing a business opportunity to participate in mandatory ethics and compliance training, and the training should include information about product and earnings claims. Appropriate disclosures should be covered to avoid implied claims related to both products and earnings. For example, when selling wellness products, distributors should be made aware of health or disease prevention claims that have not been approved through clinical trials or approved by the proper regulatory authorities. Since some distributors who sign up for the business opportunity never really engage beyond the level of personal consumption, they may not be required to engage in training. However, when certain income levels indicate the individual is pursuing a business opportunity, it is permissible to have mandatory training.

Training should also make distributors aware of the resources, support systems, and designated personnel who can assist with ethics and legal advice. The training should include actual scenarios that create the opportunity to ask questions and discuss how to navigate the risk areas relevant for a particular company. Gaining full awareness of the company's values, rules, and appropriate procedures can strengthen confidence in the ability to avoid engaging in misconduct. There should be feedback collected from the training session to determine the effectiveness of the training. This is a part of the open communication and reinforcement of the importance of responsible conduct. Additionally, it is important to guard against conducting ethics and compliance training just because it is required or to satisfy industry or regulatory standards, as the concerns for ethics and compliance need to be part of the direct selling company's ethos.

Systems to Monitor and Reinforce Compliance

Online compliance monitoring tools have been developed for direct selling companies. These tools provide effective solutions for observing and auditing the overall program's effectiveness. For example, brand-monitoring solutions can use digital alerts to learn about any reference to the company's products, brands, or overall operations in external communications. These sophisticated monitoring tools allow the compliance group to immediately address social media posts, blogs, and forums that create ethical or legal issues.

One such service provider is the Momentum Factor's FieldWatch program. Table 4.1 identifies the types of violations that FieldWatch would be screening for in the digital space. Joseph N. Mariano, president of the DSA, noted:

As the internet, mobile and social technologies give more and more people the opportunity to become involved in direct selling, it's important that we hold the digital marketing materials they increasingly use to the same high standards we set decades ago and have recently enhanced (Direct Selling Association 2016).

Additionally, artificial intelligence (AI) is being incorporated into many electronic monitoring systems to provide more accurate feedback on distributor communications and activities.

Table 4.1 Direct selling-specific violation types

- Product guarantees
- Illegal health claims
- Illegal income claim
- Brand and logo misuse
- URL squatting
- Social handle and squatting
- Marketing products and services
- Unauthorized sellers
- Checks and income images
- eBay/Amazon
- Craigslist ads
- Founder/celebrity misuse
- Employment claims
- Testimonials
- Leads and co-ops
- Social media policy
- Out-of-policy representation
- Rogue app monitoring

Source: FieldWatch (2019).

Monitoring claims on social media is an important way to locate problematic communications. This can even include using search platforms to access social media using words or phrases that relate to compliance issues. Searches often focus on the issues noted in Table 4.1. For example, during the COVID-19 pandemic, the FTC issued a number of concerns over communications from direct selling companies and distributors implying that their health and wellness products could help prevent COVID-19. Since there were no known products proven to prevent the virus, these claims quickly got the attention of, and follow-up action by, the FTC.

Encouraging distributors to report any misconduct of false earnings or product claims can be an effective way of monitoring what is happening in the field. The independent contractors should recognize that false claims jeopardize the individual's business, as well as the reputation of the direct selling company and broader community. Meetings focusing on sales success provide a great opportunity for the direct selling company to listen and learn what is going on in the field.

Enforcement and Continuous Improvement of an Ethics and Compliance Program

Program implementation translates the structure and plan into operational terms. This establishes the effectiveness of monitoring, controlling, and improving the performance of the system. The compliance function should be guided by the standards set forth by the company in conjunction with the DSA, with the legal department continually assessing relevant risks and developing policies to deal with misconduct. The effectiveness of the compliance initiatives is determined by how the company develops policies and how it structures its resources and activities to monitor and enforce.

It is important to determine appropriate enforcement responses based on the nature of the infraction. The severity of the policy violation should involve determining the intentionality of an action. Deliberate misconduct should be dealt with quickly. For example, if the distributor has engaged in a particular misconduct previously and is a repeat offender, this may indicate a willful disregard for the rules and merit much more significant consequences. On the other hand, a new distributor may not understand the rules and expectations and will need coaching that educates on appropriate conduct.

The previous chapter discussed the role of downlines in direct selling. Of great importance in ethics and compliance is the level of sales and downlines because there are business builders who have great influence and who operate in leadership positions. If training for the downline prioritizes sales volume over compliance with established rules and procedures, the company's ethics and compliance officers will need to be made aware. The officers need to be careful not to be more lenient or permissive of violations of successful distributors and business builders. Some companies have been involved in major regulatory actions because a few high-level distributors have developed and trained their downlines to use false claims and income earning potential to maximize their success. Failure to monitor and enforce policies can have significant negative consequences.

Self-Regulation of Direct Selling

Some direct selling firms choose to self-regulate their direct sales practices through membership in self-regulatory organizations. For example, many firms follow the principles of the World Federation of Direct Selling Association (WFDSA) and national-level direct selling associations such as the DSA in various countries. The WFDSA promotes ethical practices in direct selling globally through advocacy and strong relationships with governments, consumers, and academia. The various DSAs also emphasize ethical business practices and consumer protection measures and require that members adhere to the DSA's Code of Ethics.

The DSA Code of Ethics recognizes the importance of a fair and responsible approach to direct selling by:

- Prohibiting deceptive or unlawful practices regarding recruits and customers;
- Requiring that direct sellers provide accurate and truthful information about the price, quality, and promotion of the products;
- Illuminating and enforcing the need for a clear record of the sales made by contractors;
- Necessitating that warranties be fully explained;
- Requiring direct sellers to clearly identify themselves to customers and maintain the confidential information of their customers;
- Prohibiting pyramid scheme practices; and
- Providing guidelines on inventory purchases, earnings reporting, inventory loading, start-up fee payments, and training practices.

As part of the consumer protection toolkit offered by the DSA, Table 4.2 shows the specificity with which the DSA Code of Ethics guides direct selling companies, distributors, and consumers.

Table 4.2 Direct Selling Association code of ethics

As a consumer, you should expect salespeople to:

- Tell you who they are, why they're approaching you, and what products they are selling.
- Promptly end a demonstration or presentation at your request.
- Provide a receipt with a clearly stated cooling-off period permitting the consumer to withdraw from a purchase order within a minimum of three days from the date of the purchase transaction and receive a full refund of the purchase price.
- Explain how to return a product or cancel an order.
- Provide you with promotional materials that contain the address and telephone number of the direct selling company.
- Provide a written receipt that identifies the company and salesperson, including contact information for either.
- Respect your privacy by calling at a time that is convenient for you.
- Safeguard your private information.
- Provide accurate and truthful information regarding the price, quality, quantity, performance, and availability of their product or service.
- Offer a written receipt in language you can understand.
- Offer a complete description of any warranty or guarantee.

As a salesperson, you should expect a DSA member company to:

- Provide you with accurate information about the company's compensation plan, products, and sales methods.
- Describe the relationship between you and the company in writing.
- Be accurate in any comparisons about products, services, or opportunities.
- Refrain from any unlawful or unethical recruiting practice and exorbitant entrance or training fees.
- Ensure that you are not just buying products solely to qualify for downline commissions.
- Ensure that any materials marketed to you by others in the salesforce are consistent with the company's policies, are reasonably priced, and have the same return policy as the company's.
- Require you to abide by the requirements of the Code of Ethics.
- Safeguard your private information.
- Provide adequate training to help you operate ethically.
- Base all actual and potential sales and earnings claims on documented facts.
- Encourage you to purchase only the inventory you can sell in a reasonable amount of time.
- Repurchase marketable inventory and sales aids you have purchased within the past 12 months at 90 percent or more of your original cost if you decide to leave the business.
- Explain the repurchase option in writing.
- Have reasonable start-up fees and costs.

Source: Direct Selling Association (2015).

Direct Selling Association (DSA) Partners With the BBB National Programs in Self-Regulation and Monitoring

The BBB National Programs, Inc. (2019) is the home of industry self-regulatory and dispute resolution programs. The DSA and the BBB National Programs created a third-party self-regulatory program, the DSSRC, that launched in January 2019. The DSSRC monitors the entire direct selling channel, including DSA member and nonmember companies, and embodies the following principles:

- Clear industry standards on issues such as product and earning representations.
- Identification of relevant best practices from other self-regulatory models.
- Creation of a process that both monitors and enforces strict business principles.
- Enacts measures to raise the bar of excellence for DSA members and the entire direct selling channel.

These foundational aspects of the DSSRC are depicted in Figure 4.2. When a company supports the DSSRC, it demonstrates the company's commitment and leadership in supporting ethical conduct in the direct selling industry.

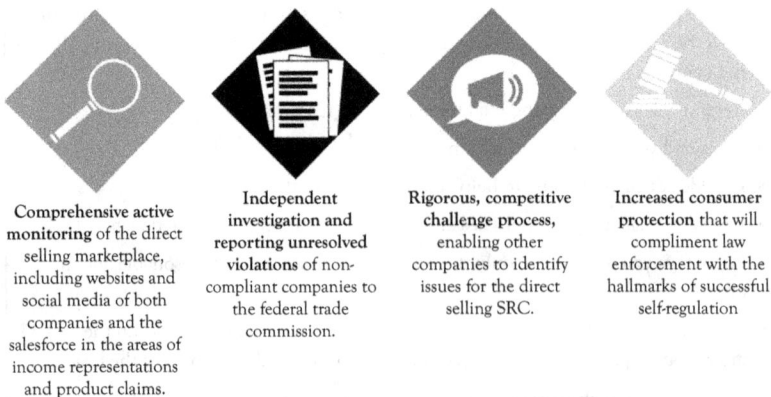

Comprehensive active monitoring of the direct selling marketplace, including websites and social media of both companies and the salesforce in the areas of income representations and product claims.

Independent investigation and reporting unresolved violations of noncompliant companies to the federal trade commission.

Rigorous, competitive challenge process, enabling other companies to identify issues for the direct selling SRC.

Increased consumer protection that will compliment law enforcement with the hallmarks of successful self-regulation

Figure 4.2 Foundational aspects of the DSSRC program

Source: Direct Selling Association (2021b). Used with permission.

Conclusion

The direct selling industry has one of the strongest regulatory systems of any direct-to-consumer marketplace. The regulatory practices exhibited through the ethics and compliance programs maintain the integrity of the direct selling channel. With organizations such as the WFDSA, DSA, and BBB National Programs promoting self-regulatory, ethical practices through strong relationships with consumers, governments, and academia, direct selling companies can focus on providing high-quality products to consumers and responsible business opportunities to aspiring entrepreneurs.

References

BBB National Programs, Inc. 2019. "The Council of Better Business Bureaus Restructures." https://bbbprograms.org/mediacenter/newsroom/cbbb_restructures#:~:text=BBB%20National%20Programs%2C%20Inc.,formerly%20administered%20by%20the%20CBBB (accessed April 22, 2021).

Direct Selling Association. 2021a. "Code Review Process." https://dsa.org/consumerprotection/code-review-process (accessed March 28, 2021).

Direct Selling Association. 2021b. "Direct Selling Self-Regulatory Council." https://dsa.org/dssrc/direct-selling-self-regulatory-council (accessed March 28, 2021).

Direct Selling Association. 2020. "DSA Growth & Outlook Report: U.S. Direct Selling in 2019." https://dsa.org/statistics-insights/overview (accessed March 21, 2021).

Direct Selling Association. 2019. "DSA/BBB National Programs, Inc. Launch Direct Selling Self-Regulatory Council." https://dsa.org/dssrc/direct-selling-self-regulatory-council (accessed March 18, 2021).

Direct Selling Association. 2016. "DSA Announces New Partnership with Momentum Factor to Bolster Code of Ethics Enforcement." https://dsa.org/events/news/individual-press-release/dsa-announces-new-partnership-with-momentum-factor-to-bolster-code-of-ethics-enforcement (accessed March 21, 2021).

Direct Selling Association. 2015. "Consumer Protection Toolkit." http://dsef.org/wp-content/uploads/2015/03/DSEF-Consumer-Protection-Toolkit.pdf (accessed March 9, 2021).

FieldWatch. 2019. "FieldWatch Compliance Management Platform." http://fieldwatchcompliance.com/ (accessed March 12, 2021).

Vesoulis, A., and E. Dockterman. 2020. "Pandemic Schemes: How Multi-Level Marketing Distributors are using the Internet—and the Coronavirus—to Grow their Businesses." *Time*, https://time.com/5864712/multilevel-marketing-schemes-coronavirus (accessed March 21, 2021).

CHAPTER 5

Direct Selling in the Global Marketplace

William F. Crittenden and Victoria L. Crittenden

Company sales growth is generated through new product offerings or geographic expansion. For direct selling companies, entering new geographic markets allows for faster revenue growth as new audiences experience a direct seller's products or services. Improvements in global telecommunications and reductions in transportation costs have created myriad opportunities for direct selling companies to increase sales, source new supplies, learn and develop new capabilities, and further differentiate products for a new set of consumers. The additional sales also contribute to the potential for economies of scale in production and overall supply chain management. Direct selling firms with a wide variety of product offerings are now obtaining a substantial share of revenues from outside their home market. A global marketplace, coupled with decreasing boundaries, has made it increasingly imperative that direct selling managers recognize and understand the phenomena that enables the forces of globalization to transform markets and create a more aggressive competitive arena.

Direct Selling Worldwide

The World Federation of Direct Selling Associations (2020) reported an estimated US$180.5 billion in 2019 worldwide direct retail sales[1]. Hester

---

[1] All data for this section is derived from the World Federation of Direct Selling Associations (2020) unless noted otherwise.

Table 5.1 Top 10 global sales for 2019

Country	2019 Retail sales (USD millions)
1. United States of America	35,210 (down 0.4% from 2018)
2. China	23,954 (down 30.0% from 2018)
3. Korea	17,683 (up 3.8% over 2018)
4. Germany	17,453 (up 5.0% over 2018)
5. Japan	15,624 (down 1.2% from 2018)
6. Brazil	9,760 (up 3.3% over 2018)
7. Malaysia	6,116 (up 5.6% over 2018)
8. Mexico	6,005 (up 2.5% over 2018)
9. France	5,184 (up 1.5% over 2018)
10. Taiwan	3,650 (down 3.9% from 2018)

Source: World Federation of Direct Selling Associations (2020).

(2020) noted the large global footprint of direct selling products and services and suggested that the direct selling business opportunity is driven by four primary global regions: Asia/Pacific, North America, South and Central America, and Europe. Supporting this assertion, Table 5.1 shows the top 10 countries in global direct sales for 2019. These 10 countries represented 78 percent of global sales (World Federation of Direct Selling Associations 2020). Overall, sales in North America and several European countries have flat-lined or declined in recent years. Additionally, the world's second largest economy, China, has recently seen a negative compound annual growth rate (CAGR) in direct selling. Alternatively, several South and Central American and Asia/Pacific country markets have demonstrated robust growth in direct selling retail sales.

Absent the decreased sales in China, where direct selling retail sales dropped 30 percent from 2018 to 2019, direct selling revenues experienced a CAGR of 1.5 percent for the years 2016–2019. The United States, with roughly 20 percent of the market, led the world in direct selling retail sales in 2019 and, in aggregate, the Americas region provided 34 percent of revenue. Mexico and Brazil have proven to be, after the United States, important direct selling markets. Yet, it is the Asia/Pacific marketplace that dominated direct selling revenue in 2019, capturing 43.7 percent of global retail sales. Predictably, despite the crackdown (discussed later in this chapter), China was the largest direct selling market in the Asia/Pacific, followed by Korea and Japan. Malaysia, despite a population ranking 42nd in the world, is the fourth largest in direct selling retail sales in the Asia/Pacific. Surprisingly, despite the large population spread over the countries of Africa and the per capita wealth of several Middle Eastern countries, these regions represent an aggregate miniscule contribution to worldwide direct selling revenues (South Africa was a notable exception within the region).

Sixty-five percent of global direct sales revenue in 2019 was driven by the two product categories of Cosmetics and Personal Care and Wellness. Table 5.2 shows the global retail sales across all product categories in 2019. Although there is still room for growth in the two largest product categories, the data suggest substantial growth opportunities in the other categories. This growth could come from improved market penetration, product diversification, or market expansion. Select country markets have already seen solid demand in some of these other categories. For example, New Zealand has experienced strong growth in Clothing and Accessories and Home Improvement, Singapore and Malaysia in Household Goods and Durables, and Korea in Foodstuffs and Beverages.

With product and market growth opportunities evident in the global marketplace, the decision to pursue international markets

Table 5.2 The 2019 global retail sales by category

Category	Percent of retail sales*
Clothing and accessories	6%
Cosmetics and personal care	29%
Home care	3%
Household goods and durables	12%
Wellness	36%
Books, toys, stationery, and so on.	2%
Foodstuff and beverages	3%
Home improvement	2%
Utilities	3%
Financial services	4%
Other	2%
*Total >100 due to rounding.	

Source: World Federation of Direct Selling Associations (2020).

should result from the direct selling firm's assessment that doing so will enhance its competitive advantage. Additionally, the benefits of global growth must exceed the costs of that growth. That is, direct selling companies will expand beyond domestic borders if that expansion results in value creation. The rationale for international expansion will vary by firm size, current product offerings, and the growth rate of the home country market.

Operating Globally

The direct selling business model and channel of distribution has a large global footprint, with almost 94 percent of worldwide direct sales and 88 percent of field sales representatives in 24 geographic markets (Hester, 2020). Even with this global footprint, growth via new market development is a viable option for direct selling firms that often see their home markets becoming saturated or stagnant or for those direct selling firms seeking to grow the overall business. van Rossum (2017) suggests five key benefits to international expansion: new markets, diversification, access to talent, competitive advantage, and foreign investment opportunities. With 95 percent of the world's consumers living outside the United States (International Trade Administration 2020), chief among these, particularly for direct selling firms, is to gain access to a larger aggregate market to grow unit sales. Additional incentives for international expansion include gaining access to new talent, developing new competencies via organizational learning (this motivation is particularly attractive for firms that base their competitive advantage on a differentiation strategy), and spreading risk over multiple economies.

However, business growth in terms of profit motivation is not the only reason for direct selling firms to grow internationally. As noted by Bennett (2010), there are a large number of entrepreneurs in developing countries operating in the informal or survival sector. Direct selling of manufactured consumer goods, with its low barriers to entry, offers a low-risk opportunity for the un(der)employed to become entrepreneurs (Dolan and Scott 2009). For example, the Deputy Minister of Economic Development of South Africa noted:

Direct selling has the potential to dramatically impact on unemployment levels in South Africa by creating thousands of jobs for youth and women ... More than simply creating jobs, direct selling provides an environment for learning, personal development and business building which are critical elements of entrepreneurship (Mkhize 2013).

Direct selling moves the micro-entrepreneur beyond the informal enterprise into being a micro-entrepreneur with the support of a larger corporation that can provide access to manufactured products, training, and development.

Additionally, there is tremendous opportunity to improve worldwide economic conditions by providing the opportunities and tools that can empower women micro-entrepreneurs (Crittenden, Crittenden, and Ajjan, 2019). Dolan and Scott (2009) and Scott, Dolan, Johnstone-Louis, Sugden, and Wu (2012) discovered that the unique nature of the direct selling marketplace provided vast opportunities for women to engage in entrepreneurial activity as a market-based solution to poverty and gender inequality. It is, therefore, not surprising that the World Federation of Direct Selling Associations (2020) indicated that women worldwide, recognizing the empowerment provided through direct selling, constitute roughly 74 percent of the direct selling salesforce.

However, just as there are both economic and social advantages for direct selling firms to operate in the global marketplace, there are also plenty of things that can, and based on Murphy's Law will, go wrong or prove challenging when running businesses in multiple countries.

Challenges With Global Direct Selling

Understanding the customer journey, recruiting and training distributors, and maintaining effective and efficient supply chains are all likely to be complex tasks for direct selling firms doing business in multiple countries. Companies expanding internationally must carefully weigh the benefits and costs of international operations and deduce that the economic value creation will ultimately exceed all costs, including opportunity costs. Expansionary direct sellers must overcome the additional costs of doing business in an unfamiliar cultural, political, and economic environment and of coordinating across geographic distances and time zones. In addition to financial risk, particularly associated with regulatory restrictions and political unease, there is the potential for a damaged reputation and loss of intellectual property.

Direct selling companies must recognize that large, well-resourced companies have stumbled when moving internationally and learn from the mistakes of others. For example, Walmart, a bricks and mortar retailer and one of the largest revenue producers in the United States, has faltered when attempting to move into large or fast-growing markets such as Germany, India, Russia, and South Korea. Translating the company's successful domestic strategy, as a low-cost leader based on superior supply chain management, proved more difficult than expected due to cultural and economic barriers. Thus, direct selling companies often rely on the assistance of more than 60 Direct Selling Associations (DSAs) worldwide to stay on top of country-related issues.

In addition to assistance provided by the country DSAs, scholars worldwide have begun to focus their research efforts on the direct selling context. A few examples of these efforts include:

- Understanding the four factors of regulating entry, educating industry participants and consumers, enforcing ethical conduct, and improving the support infrastructural environment for direct selling in Malaysia (Zain, Qureshi, and Idris 2000);
- Investigating trust in salespersons of direct selling companies in Hong Kong (Poon, Albaum, and Chan 2012);
- Examining the effectiveness of sales training in direct selling companies in Malaysia (Zaki, Rizal, Kamarudin, Husin, and Sahimi 2017);
- Considering direct selling as an alternative to traditional entrepreneurship in Spain (Avilés-Palacios, Rodríguez-Olalla, Alfonso, and García-López 2017);
- Exploring threats, impact, and future of online selling in the direct selling environment in South Africa (Wait 2019);

- Investigating the impact of information communications technology on the self-efficacy, social capital, and empowerment of women direct sellers in South Africa (Crittenden, Crittenden, and Ajjan 2019); and
- Encouraging and facilitating scholarly research on direct selling in the United States by the Direct Selling Education Foundation (2020).

Local Regulatory Restrictions

It can be extremely challenging to understand and comply with pertinent domestic and foreign country regulations for importing and exporting goods. Some countries have highly specific product standards and reporting requirements that have to be met in order to conduct sales within their borders and licensing controls for setting up business operations. Regulations can also change over time, thus requiring company management to stay apprised of changes that may affect the business either positively or adversely. Let us examine one country example where regulations have altered the direct selling landscape.

The Chinese direct sales market has seen significant growth since Avon first entered the market in 1985. However, in 2005, the Chinese government passed a law restricting a direct seller's behavior. This was in response to a somewhat unregulated environment that had resulted in pyramid selling and inadequate product information and safety. Although sales initially dropped, direct sellers responded well to these new regulations and the Chinese market again began to flourish (The Economic Times 2005). Yet, in 2019, the Chinese government decided to, once again, crack down on direct selling. Loose regulatory enforcement had allowed product counterfeiting and unsubstantiated product claims. Several direct selling companies were suspected of committing violations related to pyramid selling and failing to provide product reviews and registration in accordance with Chinese government requirements (Xuequan 2019). The founder of one domestic Chinese direct seller was sentenced to nine months in jail. Although most firms were eventually cleared of any wrongdoing, the negative publicity had a damaging impact on sales and recruiting. China's direct sales decreased by approximately 33 percent (Koe 2020).

Political and Legal Unease

The globalization of markets has taken place against a backdrop of world-wide political instability. Political stability and structural reforms are critical for longevity as an open market economy, and many emerging economies are fraught with structural issues that do not mesh well with that of advanced economic thinking. Unfortunately, terrorism is a major component of the political risk associated with international expansion (Czinkota and Ronkainen 2009). Thankfully, the global economic impact of terrorism has fallen each year and is now 77 percent lower than at its peak in 2014 (Institute for Economics & Peace 2020). However, the economic impact for 2019 was US$26 billion, indicating terrorism remains a significant problem. While a country government's aggressiveness in fighting terrorism can have a strong economic impact, companies must consider the risk associated with terrorism when making country investment decisions. Table 5.3 shows the top 25 countries experiencing negative economic impact due to terrorism.

Corruption ranks closely behind terrorism as a source of political and legal unease (Czinkota and Ronkainen 2009), and it is often viewed as a major entry barrier as firms attempt to move goods across country borders. If it is true that corruption breeds corruption (Crittenden, Hanna, and Peterson 2009) and highly corrupt countries tend to tolerate rule bending in other areas (Crittenden, Robertson, and Crittenden 2007), there are valid reasons for significant concerns about how bribery, corporate fraud, and cartels can undermine fair competition in the direct selling marketplace. The Corruption Perceptions Index ranks 180 countries and territories by their perceived levels of public sector corruption (Transparency International 2020). The 2019 index indicated that most countries have not shown much improvement in addressing corruption. Corruption was most pervasive in countries where large sums of money flow freely and where government officials appear inclined to listen only to the wealthy and well connected. Table 5.4 lists those countries receiving the lowest scores, indicating substantial corruption. Not surprisingly, most of

Table 5.3 Global terrorism index

Top countries experiencing the greatest impact from terrorist activity
1. Afghanistan
2. Iraq
3. Nigeria
4. Syria
5. Somalia
6. Yemen
7. Pakistan
8. India
9. Democratic Republic of the Congo
10. Philippines
11. Mali
12. Burkina Faso
13. Cameroon
14. Egypt
15. Mozambique
16. Libya
17. Central African Republic
18. Turkey
19. Colombia
20. Sri Lanka
21. Thailand
22. South Sudan
23. Kenya
24. Niger
25. Myanmar

Source: Institute for Economics & Peace (2020).

these countries are situated in the least economically developed regions of the globe with many also appearing on the terrorism list.

Loss of Reputation

One of a direct selling firm's most valuable intangible resources is its reputation. Indeed, many of the most highly valued firms in the world are concurrently highly ranked on reputation. The annual Global RepTrak 100 report suggests that a firm's reputation is positively affected by such factors as offering high-quality products and services, meeting customer needs, standing behind products, and behaving ethically and fairly in the way it does business (RepTrak 2020). Company or brand reputation can

Table 5.4 The corruption perceptions index

Top countries experiencing substantial corruption
1. Somalia
2. South Sudan
3. Syria
4. Yemen
5. Afghanistan
6. Sudan
7. Equatorial Guinea
8. Venezuela
9. North Korea
10. Guinea Bissau
11. Libya
12. Democratic Republic of the Congo
13. Haiti
14. Turkmenistan
15. Congo
16. Burundi
17. Iraq
18. Chad
19. Cambodia
20. Nicaragua
21. Eritrea
22. Zimbabwe
23. Madagascar
24. Tajikistan*
25. Uzbekistan*
26. Central African Republic*
27. Cameroon*
28. Comoros*
*Countries ranked 24 through 28 had identical scores.

Source: Transparency International (2020).

be the basis for a competitive advantage, and doing business globally can create significant complexity in maintaining high reputational standards. Furthermore, noncompliance with a myriad of often complex, local regulatory requirements can harm a firm's reputation. Thus, the potential for a damaged reputation must be factored into the risks and costs of engaging in direct selling worldwide.

Loss of Intellectual Property

The cost of protecting intellectual property when doing business in the global marketplace can be formidable. Large-scale patent, copyright, and trademark infringements are especially ripe in some of the fastest growing and less developed global markets. Reverse engineering, outright piracy, and product counterfeiting may allow native firms to compete at much lower costs, which will likely translate into lower prices. Decisions to source raw materials, components, or finished products may leave a firm even more vulnerable to intellectual property losses, especially regarding patents and trade secrets.

Deciding Where to Grow Globally

Direct selling companies face two key decisions when expanding into new markets—whether to customize to local preferences or whether to attempt to lower costs by achieving economies of scale. The first relates to what changes, if any, will need to be made to the company's product offerings to meet local preferences. Local responsiveness will likely increase a product's market attractiveness. Yet, altering product offerings to better fit local consumer preferences and/or host-country requirements will typically drive up costs (Prahalad and Doz 1987; Roth and Morrison 1991).

Therefore, the second key decision relates to whether or not the core driver for doing business globally is to achieve economies of scale and drive down costs. By selling the same products in both domestic and foreign markets, a direct selling company can leverage its home-based core competencies. Yet, a singular focus on cost reduction does not allow for adaptation to local preferences. Although some products may not require modification to fit different country markets, selling identical products globally may leave a firm vulnerable to an increased level of reverse engineering or piracy of intellectual property. Thus, a direct selling company's approach to cost and local responsiveness will represent strategic trade-offs.

Assuming a direct selling company has decided to compete globally, the question of where to expand needs to be well thought-out. For example, one cannot simply assume that one country market is homogenous with another because they are geographically proximate. The country selection rationale should be linked closely to the strategic drivers for expansion (e.g., access to larger market and low-cost inputs). Metrics such as country gross domestic product (GDP), GDP per capita, GDP growth, and per capita consumption of competitive products can be useful for evaluating a country's potential as a direct selling marketplace.

A country ranking based on GDP, the accumulated value of all finished goods and services produced, is an initial indicator of market attractiveness. In 2019, aggregate global GDP amounted to about US$142 trillion. Preliminary figures for 2020 suggest a 4 percent to 5 percent decrease in global GDP due to the negative economic impact of COVID-19. Economists use GDP growth in assessing the health of an economy, and financial decision makers use GDP trends to assess country market investments. Per capita GDP breaks down a country's economic output per person and is a measure for gauging the prosperity of a nation. Small countries with abundant natural resources and more developed industrial countries tend to have the highest per capita GDP.

Several countries or regions may score similarly on the aforementioned metrics (e.g., market size and growth), thus direct sellers need additional criteria for market entry decisions. One method for evaluating markets that can assist in deciding global growth options is the CAGE distance framework proposed by Ghemawat (2001). The CAGE framework integrates distance assessment in terms of [C]ultural differences, [A]dministrative and political distinctions, [G]eographic distance, and [E]conomic variance. Ghemawat suggests that overcoming greater distances, as measured by these components, will increase costs and the risks associated with a country market expansion. For example, language differences can create substantial cost obstacles in conveying marketing messages and product packing information.

Cultural Differences

Culture is composed of a collection of social norms, beliefs, and values. Cultural differences find expression in language, ethnicity, and religion. These differences frequently and directly affect customer and employee preferences. For example, the Spanish culture is not particularly entrepreneurial, with Avilés-Palacios, Rodríguez-Olalla, Alfonso, and García-López (2017) indicating that a majority of Spaniards would not pursue entrepreneurial activity due to a strong stigma associated with failure. This could explain the relatively low direct selling revenue in Spain, despite a robust population size and high unemployment. In another example, CUTCO Corporation had to alter its one-to-one business model when expanding into South Korea, due to a cultural preference for the party plan approach (Crittenden and Crittenden 1990).

There is no one measure that accurately describes the culture of a country market (or regions within a country market). In the mid-1970s, Dutch psychologist Geert Hofstede conducted some of the most significant national culture research. The framework he developed, and continued to refine through 2010, is the most widely used framework for evaluating a society's culture and its effects on societal values and behavior. Hofstede's theory posits six dimensions along which cultural differences should be considered: (1) individualism–collectivism, (2) uncertainty avoidance, (3) power distance, (4) masculinity–femininity, (5) long-term orientation, and (6) indulgence versus self-restraint (Hofstede 1980). Hofstede's research is useful as it can result in an aggregated cultural measure for each country. Managers charged with market evaluation can compare the national-culture measures for any two-country pairings to help inform entry decisions.

Similarities between two countries in language, ethnicity, religion, social norms, social networks, trust, and mutual respect will lead to lower cultural distance and thus lower entry cost. As an example, and perhaps unsurprisingly, if we compare cultural differences from the United States to Australia, Canada, Ireland, New Zealand, or the United Kingdom, the scores reflect low cultural distance. This is related, of course, to the importance of linguistic similarity. Yet, India, a country where English is highly prevalent and an official sublanguage, is found to have a much higher cultural distance from the United States due to ethnic, religious, trust, and social norm differences.

As direct selling companies begin doing business in various country economies, culture clashes can occur in a variety of areas. Furthermore, a common mistake made with global selling is assuming the culture of a country or region of the world is homogenous. For example, depending on the product, the diverse cultures of the United States (e.g., New England, Midwest, and Deep South) can alter acceptability of certain tastes or flavors and, thus, product demand. The cultural diversity of countries such as Brazil, Russia, India, and China can see similar within-border variation in product demand. As an illustration of the importance of these variations, direct selling has found its greatest acceptance as an employment opportunity in the northern and northeastern regions of India (Singh and Kumar 2019).

Administrative and Political Distinctions

Although worldwide trade barriers have generally been falling, the governments of many countries continue to maintain barriers such as tariffs, trade quotas, and foreign direct investment restrictions to protect homegrown competitors. Alternatively, those countries belonging to the same regional trading bloc see positive trade intensity. Additional administrative and political distinctions are the result of the absence of shared currency, diversity in the strength of legal and financial institutions, variation in ethics and corruption and piracy enforcement, or political hostilities. For example, those countries in the Eurozone share the same currency, have open borders, and somewhat integrate politically. As might be expected, most cross-border trade by European countries takes place within the European Union. Additionally, former colony relationships have a positive impact on bilateral trade. For example, we find strong trade between British companies and those businesses located in the commonwealth. Similarly, Spanish companies trade heavily with those from Latin American countries previously colonized by Spain.

Trade agreements can create opportunities for companies to help grow a nation's economy. These agreements provide the "rules of the road" for companies looking to do business in global markets. The goal is to reduce export barriers, while protecting a nation's interests. For example, the United States–Mexico–Canada Agreement (USMCA) (which replaced the North American Free Trade Agreement (NAFTA)) will likely have positive effects on trade and economic growth in North America. Similarly, the African Continental Free Trade Area (AfCFTA) launched at the beginning of 2021 should also have positive effects for direct sellers. The goal of AfCFTA is to reduce all trade costs and enable Africa to integrate into global supply chains by eliminating 90 percent of tariffs and creating a single market with free movement of goods and services (Kende-Robb 2021). Additionally, there has been a focused effort on the creation of self-regulatory bodies in various countries (e.g., United States and China) to ensure the integrity of direct selling principles and practice.[2]

Geographic Distance

Everyone understands that costs and risks will be associated with how far apart two countries are as measured in kilometers, miles, or nautical miles. Yet, in Ghemawat's CAGE framework, geographic distance also includes factors such as the country's time zone, whether the countries are adjacent, if the country has access via waterways, a country's physical size (e.g., physical distance between its borders), and the country's topography. A country's infrastructure (e.g., roads, railways, ports, electrical power, and telecommunications networks) also plays a role in determining geographic distance. As might be expected, inadequate or complex transportation, different climates and time zones, and unstable electrical and communication links require alterations in how firms conduct business.

Economic Variance

Per capita income and the costs and quality of natural and human resources increase the risk and cost of conducting business between two country markets. That is, wealthier countries tend to trade with other countries with high per capita income since business model repetition is easier in a country with a similar per capita income. For example, product prices that seem reasonable in countries with similar income levels might appear exorbitant to countries with lower per capita income. Interestingly, businesses located in poor countries tend to seek business expansion in wealthier countries rather than trading in other poor countries. Khanna and Palepu (2006) derived a four-tier structure of markets: (1) bottom (people who can afford only the least expensive products); (2) local (consumers happy with products of local quality and local prices); (3) glocal (consumers who want customized products of near-global standards but are not willing to pay the global standard price); and (4) global

---

[2] Chapter 4 provides more detail on ethics and compliance in direct selling.

(consumers who want products of same quality as that found in developed countries and who are willing to pay global prices).

Attractiveness of Emerging Markets

Globalization has recently undergone some retrenchment with a stronger focus on country nationalism. Rather than multinational trade deals negotiated by international bodies such as the World Trade Organization, bilateral treaties between countries are in vogue. The Brexit experience demonstrates the fragility of economic trading blocs and the unexpected consequences from exiting. It remains to be seen whether such sentiments will have a lasting impact, yet it is clear that entry barriers are lower for many emerging country markets.

Crittenden and Crittenden (2010) described emerging economies as low-income, rapid-growth countries that are using economic liberalization as the primary engine of growth. Two significant trends exist within the external environment of the global marketplace that have a significant impact on the business transactions within an emerging economy. These trends are demography and technology.

Demographic Trends

A country's demographics have a direct effect on its economy as a country moves toward global economic growth and development[3]. Nine of the 10 countries with the highest populations in the world are in the emerging market space. These include (in order of size): China, India, Indonesia, Pakistan, Brazil, Nigeria, Bangladesh, Russia, and Mexico. (Interestingly, China's population is projected to decline by around 350 million by 2100; Gramlich 2019.) Nine of the 10 countries expected to experience the greatest population growth by 2100 are in emerging markets. Eight of the 10 are in Africa, including Nigeria, the Democratic Republic of the Congo, Tanzania, Ethiopia, Angola, Niger, Egypt, and Sudan. Additionally, the population within South Africa is expected to increase 12

---

[3] Unless noted otherwise, all statistics derived in this section are from the Population Reference Bureau (2008).

percent between 2008 and 2050. The expanding wealth accompanying these growing populations has been, and will continue to be, a powerful driver of growth in many sectors.

Yet, the demographic divide, the measure of the inequality in the population and health profiles usually assessed between rich and poor countries, is evident within emerging economy countries. For example, while both India and China have pockets of prosperity, the national wealth is distributed unevenly with most of the population in the two countries living in severe poverty (Wharton 2008). Economists also talk about the demographic dividend, the boost in economic growth that can result from changes in a country's population age structure. In other words, "As fertility rates decrease, a country's working-age population grows larger relative to the young dependent population. With more people in the labor force and fewer children to support, a country has a window of opportunity for rapid economic growth if the right social and economic investments and policies are made in health, education, governance, and the economy" (Johns Hopkins University 2021). According to Crittenden and Crittenden (2012, 572), "An emerging market that is currently partaking of its demographic dividend will need governance issues related to an aging work force compared to an emerging market that has yet to enter into the demographic dividend. A market with high piracy rates and a large demographic divide will need a different governance framework than one with a large middle class and almost 100 percent mobile phone penetration."

Technological Developments

Technology growth has served to integrate emerging economies into the global marketplace at an unprecedented pace. Countries and businesses are working to create a technological infrastructure that should portend well for these emerging markets. The adoption and use of technology in emerging markets create an interesting opportunity to better understand critical drivers of competitive advantage. Thinking creatively about technological linkages and their implications within and across emerging and advanced economies is imperative for future marketplace success (Crittenden and Crittenden 2010).

Technology can bring structural changes to economies and is a primary driver of productivity growth and living standards. Direct selling companies operating in emerging markets could use technology to create new markets and expand product and service offerings to unserved and underserved members of the community. Not only are new customers acquired, new sellers are gained to serve these markets. With technology playing a central role in emerging market development, direct selling companies can help transform the pursuit of profits into a driver of economic growth that will result in higher productivity and improved living standards.

In Africa, for example, a report by the International Finance Corporation (2018, 8) noted, "the availability of faster Internet via undersea fiber optic cable has contributed to a reduction in inequality, the creation of new business models, and the generation of new jobs that provide new opportunities for unskilled workers to climb the economic ladder." In his exploration of the adoption of technology among direct sellers in South Africa, Wait (2019) queried independent salespeople from 13 of South Africa's DSA member companies. Overall, the feedback reflected a positive attitude toward the development of technology in direct selling and felt that advancement of technology was a necessity for direct selling companies to succeed in the country. Based on their research in Germany, Neatu and Imbriscă (2016) suggested that direct sellers simply do not have the manpower to reach all regional areas and would need to build out their e-commerce business to accomplish better market penetration.

Strategic Implications for Direct Selling Globally

Because of increasing global integration in products and services as well as capital markets, the benefits of competing globally outweigh the costs for more and more enterprises. Even small- and medium-size enterprises are able to leverage lower trade barriers, reduce logistical costs, and utilize technology to compete successfully beyond their home market. Yet, global direct selling does not come without challenges and managers need to decide if, and how, the firm should compete beyond its home market.

When making a global expansion decision, direct selling company leaders have a number of methodologies to aid in international expansion decisions. The CAGE distance framework, for example, allows cultural, administrative and political, geographic, and economic assessment for any potential country pairing. Recognizing the strategic trade-offs, direct selling managers also must decide if new market entry globally will allow for the sales of identical products or if global direct selling will require adaptation to local preferences.

Concurrently, consideration must be given to the degree of investment and desired level of control when doing business globally. Adequate investment funding is necessary to ensure successful market entry. Obviously, direct selling firms need funding for recruiting and training distributors and for in-country operational concerns. Direct selling companies must be prepared to sustain losses or breakeven operations when first entering a new global market. However, the data suggest there are untapped markets in the global sphere for direct selling success.

References

Avilés-Palacios, C., A. Rodríguez-Olalla, J.G. Alfonso, and M.J. García-López. 2017. "Direct Selling, A Possible Type of Entrepreneurship." *Transylvanian Review* XXV, no. 19, pp. 4876–4883.

Bennett, J. 2010. "Informal Firms in Developing Countries: Entrepreneurial Stepping Stone or Consolation prize." *Small Business Economics*, 34, no. 1, pp. 53–63.

Crittenden, W.F., and V.L. Crittenden. 2002. "CUTCO International." In *Strategic Marketing Management Cases*, eds. D.W. Cravens, C.W. Lamb, and V.L. Crittenden, 7th ed., 558–572. Burr Ridge, IL: McGraw-Hill Irwin.

Crittenden, V.L., and W.F. Crittenden. 2010. "Strategic Management in Emerging Economies: A Research Agenda." *Organizations and Markets in Emerging Economies* 1, no. 1, pp. 9–23.

Crittenden, V.L., and W.F. Crittenden. 2012. "Corporate Governance in Emerging Economies: Understanding the Game." *Business Horizons* 55, no. 6, pp. 567–576.

Crittenden, V.L., W.F. Crittenden, and H. Ajjan. 2019. "Empowering Women Micro-Entrepreneurs in Emerging Economies: The Role of Information Communications Technology." *Journal of Business Research* 98, pp. 191–203.

Crittenden, V., R. Hanna, and R. Peterson. 2009. "Business Students' Attitudes toward Unethical Behavior: A Multi-Country Comparison." *Marketing Letters* 20, no. 1, pp. 1–14.

Crittenden, W., C. Robertson, and V. Crittenden. 2007. "Hard Facts about Software Piracy." *Business Strategy Review* 18, no. 4, pp. 30–33.

Czinkota, M., and I. Ronkainen. 2009. "Trends and Indications in International Business: Topics for Future Research." *Management International Review* 49, no. 2, pp. 249–265.

Direct Selling Education Foundation. 2020. https://dsef.org/ (accessed February 15, 2021).

Dolan, C., and L. Scott. 2009. "Lipstick Evangelism: Avon Trading Circles and Gender Empowerment in South Africa." *Gender & Development* 17, no. 2, pp. 203–218.

Ghemawat, P. 2001. "Distance still Matters: The Hard Reality of Global Expansion." *Harvard Business Review* 79, no. 8, pp. 137–147.

Gramlich, J. 2019. "For World Population Day, A Look at the Countries with the Biggest Projected Gains – and Losses – by 2100." *Pew Research Center*, https://pewresearch.org/fact-tank/2019/07/10/for-world-population-day-a-look-at-the-countries-with-the-biggest-projected-gains-and-losses-by-2100/ (accessed January 29, 2021).

Hester, G.D. 2020. *Positioned Right*. Sarasota, FL: Hester Consulting Services, LLC.

Hofstede, G. 1980. *Culture's Consequences: International Differences in Work-Related Values*. Beverly Hills, CA: Sage.

Institute for Economics & Peace. 2020. "Global Terrorism Index 2020: Measuring the Impact of Terrorism." https://economicsandpeace.org (accessed February 14, 2021).

International Finance Corporation. 2018. "How Technology Creates Markets: Trends and Examples for Private Investors in Emerging Markets." p. 8. https://openknowledge.worldbank.org/handle/10986/30196 (accessed February 15, 2021).

International Trade Administration. 2020. "The International Trade Administration granting Relief to U.S. Companies during Covid-10 Response." https://trade.gov/press-release/international-trade-administration-granting-relief-us-companies-during-covid-19 (accessed February 14, 2021).

Johns Hopkins University. 2021. "Demographic Dividend – Investing in Human Capital." https://demographicdividend.org/ (accessed February 15, 2021).

Kende-Robb, C. 2021. "6 Reasons why Africa's New Free Trade Area is a Game Changer." *World Economic Forum*, https://weforum.org/agenda/2021/02/afcfta-africa-free-trade-global-game-changer/ (accessed February 15, 2021).

Khanna, T., and K.G. Palepu. 2006. "Emerging Giants: Building World-Class Companies in Developing Countries." *Harvard Business Review* 84, no. 10, pp. 60–69.

Koe, T. 2020. "Direct-Selling Firms in China look to New Retail Channels amid Tough Market Environment." https://nutraingredients-asia.com/Article/2020/02/10/Direct-selling-firms-in-China-look-to-new-retail-channels-amid-tough-market-environment (accessed January 24, 2021).

Neatu, A.M., and C.I. Imbriscă. 2016. "An Overview of the Direct Selling Industry." *Annals of Faculty of Economics, University of Oradea, Faculty of Economics* 1, no. 1, pp. 987–994.

Poon, P., G. Albaum, and P.S.F. Chan. 2012. "Managing Trust in Direct Selling Relationships." *Marketing Intelligence & Planning*, 30, no. 5, pp. 588–603.

Prahalad, C.K., and Y.L. Doz. 1987. *The Multinational Mission*. New York, NY: Free Press.

Roth, K., and A.J. Morrison. 1991. "An Empirical Analysis of the Integration-Responsiveness Framework in Global Industries." *Journal of International Business Studies* 21, pp. 541–564.

RepTrak. 2020. "Global RepTrak – 2020's Most Reputable Companies Worldwide." https://reptrak.com/global-reptrak-100/ (accessed February 14, 2021).

Scott, L., C. Dolan, M. Johnstone-Louis, K. Sugden, and M. Wu. 2012. "Enterprise and Inequality: A Study of Avon in South Africa." *Entrepreneurship Theory and Practice* 36, no. 3, pp. 543–568.

Singh, N.K., and S. Kumar. 2019. "Direct Selling: Understanding Its Building Blocks and Current Status in India." *International Journal of Research and Analytical Reviews* 6, no. 1, 488–495.

The Economic Times. 2005. "China Lifts Ban on Direct Selling." https://economictimes.indiatimes.com/china-lifts-ban-on-directselling/articleshow/1219135.cms (accessed February 14, 2021).

Transparency International. 2020. "Corruption Perceptions Index 2020." https://transparency.org/cpi (accessed February 14, 2021).

van Rossum, J.E. 2017. "5 Benefits of International Expansion." https://bizjournals.com/bizjournals/how-to/growth-strategies/2017/12/5-benefits-of-international-expansion.html (accessed February 14, 2021).

Wait, M. 2019. "The Rivalry Between Online and Direct Selling – Is There a Winner?" *Acta Commercii – Independent Research Journal in Management Science*, 19, no. 1. https://doi.org/10.4102/ac.v19i1.679 (accessed February 15, 2021).

Wharton. 2008. "When Are Emerging Markets No Longer 'Emerging?'" Knowledge@Wharton, http://knowledge.wharton.upenn.edu/article.cfm?articleid=1911 (accessed January 15, 2012).

World Federation of Direct Selling Associations. 2020. "Global Direct Selling—2019 Retail Sales." https://wfdsa.org/wp-content/uploads/2020/07/Sales-Seller-2020-Report-Final.pdf (accessed February 13, 2021).

Xuequan, M. 2019. "Registered Direct Selling Products in China Nearly Cut in Half: MOC." http://xinhuanet.com/english/2019-06/10/c_138131792.htm (accessed January 24, 2021).

Zain, O., Z.A. Quraeshi, and M.A. Idris. 2000. "Direct Selling in Malaysia." *Journal of Asia-Pacific Business*, 2, no. 4, pp. 83–101.

Zaki, E.B.E.M., A.M. Rizal, S. Kamarudin, M.M. Husin, and M. Sahimi. 2017. "Effective Sales Training in a Direct Selling Organization." *Journal of Computational and Theoretical Nanoscience* 23, no. 4, pp. 3021–3024.

CHAPTER 6

On the Benefits of Direct Selling

Robert A. Peterson

From a macromarketing perspective, direct selling is a business model or a channel of distribution for consumer products and services. Simultaneously, from a micromarketing perspective, direct selling is face-to-face selling activity away from a fixed retail location (e.g., Peterson and Wotruba 1996). According to the Direct Selling Association (2020), 6.8 million individuals were classified as "active direct sellers" in the United States in 2019. Of the active direct sellers, 13 percent were classified as full-time direct sellers, whereas 87 percent were classified as part-time direct sellers. Virtually all direct sellers are independent contractors, not employees of direct selling companies, and about three-quarters of direct sellers are women. As such, direct selling is part of the so-called gig economy.

This chapter attempts to answer the quasi-rhetorical question, "Why do people become direct sellers, and what are the possible benefits accruing to direct sellers as a result of their direct selling experience?" Broadly speaking, there are two categories of possible reasons for becoming a direct seller: financial and nonfinancial. Financial benefits are writ large: people become direct sellers because of monetary or economic rewards received from their direct selling activities. However, it is possible that people become direct sellers for nonfinancial reasons and benefits that are more subtle and nuanced than financial reasons and benefits. Such reasons relate to (but are not limited to) opportunities for social interactions, personal learning and growth, and feelings of accomplishment. Specifically, this chapter seeks answers to three questions:

- Why do people become direct sellers?
- What do direct sellers expect to earn when they enter the gig economy, and what do they actually earn from their "direct selling gig?"
- Does a direct selling experience improve an individual's personal life skills?

To provide an introductory context for addressing these questions, the next section presents reflections provided by three women regarding their respective direct selling experiences, two current direct sellers and one former direct seller. The remainder of the chapter conveys the results of two empirical surveys designed to produce at least preliminary answers to the three questions. In particular, the following section discusses the results of a nationwide survey of gig workers regarding their reasons for entering the gig economy, with an emphasis on the expected and actual financial rewards of gig workers who are direct sellers. By definition, and as discussed later, direct sellers constitute a subset of gig workers. Hence, it is instructive to compare the characteristics and motivations of direct sellers with those of other gig workers. The subsequent section contains observations based on a separate nationwide survey of direct sellers regarding the reasons they became direct sellers and the ensuing nonfinancial benefits that they acquired as a result of their direct selling experience. The chapter concludes with a discussion of the collective survey results and their implications.

Three Direct Selling Experiences

To complement the survey findings and provide a personal perspective on benefits derived from a direct selling experience, direct selling reflections were solicited from three geographically dispersed female direct sellers. The first is a woman who sells cosmetics; the second sells women's clothing; and the third is a former direct seller who sold household products. The direct seller who sells cosmetics is a "career direct seller" who has worked more than three decades in direct selling. The second, who sells women's clothing, has been a direct seller for about three years. The third is a former direct seller who sold household products for two years. The reflections are free-form and essentially verbatim (with minor edits).

Although the reflections are those of only three individuals, collectively they illustrate several direct selling benefits and are consistent with prior research findings on direct selling as well as the survey findings presented in this chapter.

Direct Seller One

My [direct selling] career has been life-changing and has resulted in a very close and loving family as we have been able to spend so much time together because of career flexibility. The relationships I have been able to form all over the United States and Canada are the most trusting and loving I could ever imagine. I definitely feel confident in front of large audiences as a result of my direct selling activities. I look forward to getting up at 5 am or earlier to plan my work and work my plan. I don't ever want to retire because my career is so rewarding, and I love the energy it gives me and the challenges and opportunities it provides. I especially enjoy enriching the lives of others and love watching how their lives have changed.

Among the things I learned from direct selling was to make a list of the six most important things I will do tomorrow before I go to bed at night and post the weekly schedule on the refrigerator. Soon my children were making lists. Everyone in our family knew the important activities as they were posted on the refrigerator. We even planned a family night when we would go out to eat once a week and let each family member talk about issues or events that were important to them. When the children were small, I would kiss them goodbye and tell them not to disturb me unless it was an emergency (which meant blood) and I would see them in one hour so that I could make my sales phone calls uninterrupted while their father or a caregiver would be with them. My children learned to respect my business, and my clients were able to have my undivided attention.

Direct Seller Two

Having my own (direct selling) business allows me to be in charge of my calendar and to work as much or as little as I want and set my office hours and my availability to do shows. That being said, my time management skills have been sharpened because I know how to better say "yes" and sometimes "no." My organization skills have improved as my sales volume has increased. I am constantly juggling orders, handling customer returns/exchanges, communicating with (and coaching) my show hostesses, sending follow-up e-mails to clients, and keeping on top of marketing efforts.

My presentation skills have improved because there is now a "script" for me to follow and it helps me to stay within the desired presentation window. Of course, I can add my own verbiage so that I don't sound too scripted and I like to make sure to interject some humor as well. I am more comfortable in front of a group of people and feel like I can keep them engaged throughout.

My focus is on developing relationships with my clients so therefore I have learned to ask more questions and listen for cues and talk less about myself! As a result, I am able to better serve my clients, help them make better product choices and increase their confidence. I'm also able to empathize with my clients' frustrations of traditional shopping (and the overwhelming shopping choices online) and offer a real solution to their product needs.

Former Direct Seller

I use [company] to explain how my life pivoted from being a shy individual who lacked confidence to the outspoken strong success-ful confident woman I am today. As a result of [company] training, direct selling program, and management support, I gained the skills, strength, and confidence to not only speed through promotions but also to handle my family situation! I was able to successfully turn a neg-ative situation into a positive one in my life. I am also thankful for the additional opportunities presented by [company]. Because I excelled as a direct selling representative, I had a fantastic experience that shaped the beginning of my career in sales. The skills I gained from [company] helped me with interviews, sales positions, and everyday life! Thank you [company] for creating an opportunity that changed my life in a positive manner!

The Gig Worker Survey

At its essence, the gig economy is a heterogeneous collection of firms and individuals—"gig workers" or "on-demand workers"—engaged in a wide variety of ad hoc or short-term activities and tasks (e.g., Benoit, Baker, Bolton, Gruber, and Kandampully 2017; Duszynski 2020). Gig workers range from an Uber driver to a freelance artist to a day laborer who waits on a street corner to be picked up for that day's work to a direct seller. Researchers (e.g., Kuhn and Maleki 2017) have variously labeled gig workers as independent contractors, freelancers, sellers, partners, micro-entrepreneurs, and so on, all terms that reasonably apply to direct sellers. In general, regardless of their specific gig(s), individuals who work in the gig economy do so "to earn a little extra money" and have "freedom to work from wherever they want."

To obtain empirical data about the reasons why people become direct sellers and the financial rewards that direct sellers seek and obtain, 2,210 members of a large, nationwide (USA) Internet-based consumer panel were contacted.[1] These panel members were randomly selected and, after appropriate quality-control screening, asked to read the following definition of a gig: "A gig is defined as a flexible work arrangement that allows a person to work how, when, and where he or she wants to work. Even full-time and part-time employees may sometimes work gigs in their free time." Eight examples of gigs were provided to contextualize the definition, such as "skill-based services (home repair, yard maintenance, house cleaning);" "ridesharing, transportation services;" and "professional services (accounting, law, consulting, graphic design, photography)." Included among the examples, and the focus of this chapter, was "selling products through a direct selling or network marketing business."

After reading the definition and examples, panel members were asked whether they have "worked a gig in the past 12 months." A total of 1,001 panel members, approximately 45 percent of those asked, indicated that they had worked a gig in the 12 months preceding the survey (i.e., the

---

[1] This section of the chapter is based on research conducted for the Ultimate Gig Project (Fleming 2021).

time period was July 2019–June 2020). These individuals constituted a sample of self-identified gig workers. Approximately 51 percent of these gig workers (survey participants) consisted of males, 35 percent were 18 to 34 years of age, 39 percent were 35 to 54 years of age, and 26 percent were 55 years of age or older. Fifty-four percent of the survey participants were married. Forty-seven states in the USA and the District of Columbia were represented in the sample.

Survey participants reporting they had worked a gig in the 12 months preceding the survey were first asked how many gigs they had worked. Then, depending on whether they had worked one or more than one gig, they were presented with a list of 14 gig types (plus an "other") and asked to indicate the type of gig they had worked (as their only, primary, or primary and secondary gigs). Approximately 8.7 percent of the survey participants stated that their only (2.6 percent), primary (2.9 percent), or secondary (3.2 percent) gig was "selling/representing products through a direct selling or network marketing business." (As an aside, it is noteworthy that more than two-thirds of the direct sellers worked more than one gig.) To avoid possible confounding due to differences between an only/primary direct selling gig and a secondary direct selling gig, only survey participants who stated their only/primary gig was direct selling (55 individuals or 5.5 percent of the total sample) were the focus of this chapter.[2]

In general, relatively fewer direct sellers than other gig workers considered their gig to be part-time (62 percent of direct sellers versus 73 percent of other gig workers). All survey participants were asked to think back to when they first started working their gig. Specifically, they were presented with 16 reasons for entering the gig economy and asked the extent to which they agreed or disagreed that each reason influenced their decision to enter the gig economy. The most important reason people entered the gig economy was "I wanted to make a little extra money." This was true for both direct sellers and other gig workers; 75 percent of each group agreed that this was a reason for entering the gig economy.

---

[2] Because of the relatively small number of direct sellers in the sample, caution must be exercised when attempting to broadly generalize any findings based on them.

Other important reasons people entered the gig economy include "I wanted to enjoy both work and life more" and "I wanted freedom to work from wherever I want." The least important reason people gave for entering the gig economy was "I wanted to receive a discount on products or services;" 31 percent of the survey participants agreed that this was a reason for joining the gig economy. However, interestingly enough, direct sellers were significantly more likely than other gig workers to state that they entered the gig economy to receive a discount on products or services; 46 percent of the direct sellers agreed with this reason as compared with 30 percent of other gig workers. Direct sellers were also significantly more likely than other gig workers to have entered the gig economy to be part of a supportive group or community.

To explore the financial rewards associated with various gigs, all survey participants were asked three questions:

- When you started your gig, how much money did you expect to earn?
- How much do you earn from your gig? and
- What percent of your total household income comes from gig work?

Tables 6.1 to 6.3 respectively provide answers to these questions. Table 6.1 reveals that more than 7 out of 10 direct sellers (71 percent) expected to earn less than US$500 per month when they entered the gig economy. This is slightly more than the 66 percent of other gig workers who expected to earn less than US$500 per month when entering the gig economy.

Table 6.1 Expected monthly gig income

	Percentage response	
Expected income	**Direct sellers**	**Other gig workers**
Less than US$100	25.5	22.7
US$100–US$299	23.6	24.9
US$300–US$499	21.8	18.4
US$500–US$999	9.1	14.4
US$1,000–US$1,999	9.1	9.5
US$2,000 or more	10.9	10.1

Table 6.2 *Actual gig monthly income*

Actual income	Percentage response	
	Direct sellers	Other gig workers
Less than US$100	25.5	20.0
US$100–US$299	23.6	26.9
US$300–US$499	23.6	17.2
US$500–US$999	7.3	15.3
US$1,000–US$1,999	14.5	10.4
US$2,000 or more	5.5	10.2

Table 6.2 reveals that, in general, both direct sellers and other gig workers actually earn about the same amount or more than they expected to earn. More specifically, based on a cross-tabulation of responses to the income categories in Tables 6.1 and 6.2, 80 percent of the direct sellers stated that they earned as much or more than they expected to earn when entering the gig economy. This compares with 85 percent of other gig workers.

Table 6.3 contains answers to the question regarding the percentage of total household income due to gig work. The table indicates that a plurality of both direct sellers and other gig workers earn less that 10 percent of their household income from gig work.

When asked how they primarily use the money earned from their gig, direct sellers and other gig workers displayed somewhat different spending patterns. To illustrate, whereas 31 percent of the direct sellers use their gig earnings to pay household bills, 37 percent of other gig workers use their gig earnings to pay household bills. Furthermore, whereas

Table 6.3 *Gig income as a percent of household income*

Percent of income	Percentage response	
	Direct sellers	Other gig workers
Less than 10%	40.0	46.3
10%–24%	32.7	20.8
25%–49%	18.2	15.6
50%–74%	7.3	8.4
75%–100%	1.8	8.9

26 percent of the direct sellers use their gig earnings to improve their personal lifestyle, 15 percent of other gig workers use their gig earnings in this fashion. Moreover, whereas 22 percent of the direct sellers save or invest their gig earnings, the corresponding percentage for other gig workers is 31 percent.

Finally, to assess overall reactions to their gigs, survey participants were asked two closed-end questions: "How would you rate your overall experience working your gig?" and "How likely are you to recommend your gig to a friend or colleague?" When considered together, these questions address survey participants' satisfaction with their gig. Response categories for the first question ranged from "very positive" to "very negative." Response categories for the second question ranged from "not at all likely" to "extremely likely."

Approximately 93 percent of the direct sellers viewed their experience as either "very" (49 percent) or "somewhat" (44 percent) positive. This compares with 52 percent of the other gig workers who viewed their experience as "very positive" and 35 percent who viewed it as "somewhat positive" (which total to approximately 87 percent). When asked how likely they were to recommend their gig to a friend or colleague, 66 percent of the direct sellers and 65 percent of the other gig workers stated they were either "very likely" or "extremely likely" to do so. Thus, while slightly more direct sellers than other gig workers were satisfied with their gig experience, the likelihood of recommending their gig to a friend or colleague was virtually identical for direct sellers and other gig workers.

The Direct Seller Survey

This section of the chapter reports findings based on research conducted by Peterson, Albaum, and Crittenden (2019) and Peterson, Crittenden, and Albaum (2020). These researchers studied a sample of direct sellers by surveying members of a large, nationwide (USA) Internet-based consumer panel. (The gig worker and direct seller surveys were independent and conducted at different times.) All selected Internet panel members successfully passing quality-control screening read the following definition of direct selling:

Direct Selling is defined as a channel of distribution for personally selling products directly to consumers away from a fixed retail location. **Direct selling** includes sales made through one-on-one demonstrations, a party plan, and other personal contact arrangements as well as Internet sales. **Direct selling** occurs at home, at work, and in other nonstore locations.

After reading this definition, panel members were asked: "Are you currently an independent contractor (i.e., an independent associate) for a direct selling company?" Panel members who answered "yes" to this question constituted a sample of 495 self-identified direct sellers.

Approximately 69 percent of the direct sellers were females; 75 percent worked for a direct selling company that is commonly termed a network marketing company or a multilevel marketing company.[3] Sixty percent were married. Thirty-seven percent were 18 to 34 years of age, 39 percent were 35 to 54 years of age, and 26 percent were 55 years of age or older. Forty-six states in the USA were represented in the sample. Eighty percent of the direct sellers stated that they also had a job other than direct selling. Comparison of the demographic characteristics of gig workers in general with those of direct sellers corroborates a conclusion that direct sellers are merely a subset of gig workers. It is noteworthy that even though proportionately more than twice as many women as men tend to be direct sellers, significantly more male direct sellers than female direct sellers—54 percent versus 31 percent—want direct selling to be their "full-time gig."

Direct sellers were presented with a list of 12 possible reasons for joining their current direct selling company and asked to indicate which, if any, of the reasons applied to them. The reason with the largest agreement percentage was "I believed that the products are of such value that I wanted to share them with my friends, neighbors, and the public." Eighty-one percent of the direct sellers stated that this was a reason they joined their current direct selling company. The second most frequently cited reason was "I wanted to buy the company's product(s) for myself and/or family

---

[3] Technically, multilevel marketing (MLM) is a type of compensation, not a form of direct selling.

at a discount;" 74 percent of the direct sellers stated this was a reason for joining their current direct selling company. The third- and fourth-most cited reasons were "flexible working hours" and "needed the income." The least-frequently mentioned reason direct sellers gave for joining their current direct selling company was "I wanted a full-time working career." Thirty-five percent gave this as a reason; this finding reinforces the notion that direct selling should be characterized as gig work.

Although the reasons direct sellers gave for joining their current direct selling company were fairly consistent across demographic characteristics, a few significant differences were observed between male and female direct sellers. These differences can be interpreted as suggesting that male direct sellers tend to seek more financial and business-oriented benefits than do female direct sellers, whereas female direct sellers tend to be relatively more motivated by the social aspects of direct selling.

Personal Life Self-Efficacy and Direct Selling

Beyond providing overt financial benefits, direct selling can provide non-financial benefits. In particular, the direct seller survey documented that a direct selling experience can enhance or facilitate personal self-efficacy, separately from any financial benefits received. Self-efficacy is "the belief in one's capabilities to organize and to execute the courses of action required to produce given attainments" (Bandura 1997, 2). As such, self-efficacy reflects the *confidence* that one has regarding his or her abilities to accomplish certain goals or undertake specific activities. It does not reflect the *ability* to actually accomplish the goals or carry out the activities. Even so, in a sales context, research has shown that the greater a salesperson's self-efficacy, the more superior his or her sales performance is (e.g., Peterson 2020). Unlike a personality trait, self-efficacy is more akin to a psychological state that is specific to a particular goal, task, or activity domain. Consequently, self-efficacy is malleable, that is, it can be, at least theoretically, enhanced or degraded through, among other mechanisms, personal experience gained from direct selling.

Among other questions, the direct sellers were presented with a series of 13 statements regarding personal life skills and asked to indicate the extent to which "you agree or disagree that you have benefitted from your direct selling experience in terms of improved ... skills." Because these statements reflect perceived personal life skill benefits, they, individually and collectively represent measures of self-efficacy. Agreement/disagreement was captured by means of four-point rating scales having response categories "strongly disagree," "somewhat disagree," "somewhat agree," and "strongly agree." Specifically, the direct sellers were asked, "Apart from direct selling, to what extent have you benefitted from your selling experience in terms of your personal life? In other words, to what extent have you been able to transfer skills learned from your direct selling experience to your personal life?"

In addition, direct sellers who stated they had a job other than direct selling were asked whether they agreed or disagreed with the statement: "Because of my direct selling experience, I perform better in other, non-direct selling jobs" using a four-category rating scale ranging from "strongly disagree" to "strongly agree." Of these direct sellers (80 percent of all direct sellers surveyed), 84 percent either somewhat or strongly agreed with the statement, illustrating that the "lessons learned" from a direct selling experience can carry over and enhance performance of nondirect selling jobs.

Table 6.4 presents the 13 personal life skill statements that were analyzed, the percentages of direct sellers indicating agreement or disagreement with each statement, and the mean agreement (average rating scale response) for each statement. The mean serves as a summary statistic of agreement. The larger the mean, the more the direct sellers believed that their direct selling experience was beneficial with respect to that skill. Note that a direct "test" of self-efficacy ("I enhanced my self-esteem") was embedded among the statements as a check on survey validity. Across the 13 personal life skills studied, a minimum of 74 percent of the direct sellers strongly or somewhat agreed that their direct selling experience enhanced each of them. Slightly more direct sellers believed that their listening skills and their confidence were most improved by their direct selling experience; 83 percent of the direct sellers somewhat or strongly agreed that these skills benefitted the most from their direct selling experience.

Table 6.4 Personal life skills benefitting from direct selling experience

Life Skill	Percentage Response			
	Strongly Disagree	Somewhat Disagree	Somewhat Agree	Strongly Agree
I feel more at ease in front of an audience (Mean = 2.99)	8	17	43	32
I improved my decision-making skills (Mean = 3.07)	6	13	49	32
I am better at communicating with groups (Mean = 3.05)	6	16	46	32
I am better at time management (Mean = 3.06)	6	14	48	32
I am better at managing my finances (Mean = 3.00)	6	18	46	30
I enhanced my self-esteem (Mean = 3.08)	7	14	44	35
I enhanced my confidence (Mean = 3.08)	6	11	50	33
I am better at interpersonal relationships (Mean = 3.04)	6	15	49	30
I am better at coping with and managing stress (Mean = 2.96)	7	19	46	28
I am better at problem solving (Mean = 3.08)	6	13	46	35
I improved my entrepreneurial skills (Mean = 3.09)	6	12	48	34
I enhanced my critical thinking ability (Mean = 3.00)	7	15	49	29
I improved my listening skills (Mean = 3.13)	5	12	48	35

Source: Peterson (2018).

It is perhaps not surprising that there was a significant positive relationship between responses to each of the 13 personal life skill statements and responses to the self-perceived nonsales job performance rating scale. That is, the greater the perceived personal skill benefit (perceived nonsales job performance) resulting from a direct selling experience, the greater the perceived nonsales job performance (perceived personal skill benefit). These relationships are consistent with what has been found in prior self-efficacy—sales performance research (but begs the question whether there is a causal relationship between the two).

There were generally no significant differences in reported personal life skill benefits obtained from a direct selling experience between urban and rural direct sellers or among direct sellers with different lengths of time working with their current direct selling company. Similarly, there were generally only minor differences between millennials and nonmillennials with respect to personal life skills acquired from a direct selling experience. Even so, relatively more millennials than nonmillennials reported that their direct selling experience helped them improve their interpersonal relationships (87 percent versus 75 percent) and made them more able to cope with and manage stress in their personal lives (81 percent versus 70 percent).

However, there were differences between male and female direct sellers with respect to perceived personal life skill benefits due to a direct selling experience. Male direct sellers were proportionally more likely than female direct sellers to believe that improvements in 8 of the 13 personal life skills occurred because of their direct selling experience. Thus, for example, whereas 88 percent of the male direct sellers believed that their direct selling experience enhanced their critical thinking ability, 74 percent of the female direct sellers held this belief. In brief, male and female direct sellers reported several proportionally different personal life skill benefits (with male direct sellers always more positive than female direct sellers):

- Enhanced critical thinking ability (88 percent versus 74 percent).
- Better at coping with and managing stress (85 percent versus 69 percent).
- Better at problem solving (90 percent versus 76 percent).
- Feel more at ease in front of an audience (84 percent versus 71 percent).
- Better at time management (87 percent versus 77 percent).

- Improved entrepreneurial skills (90 percent versus 78 percent).
- Improved decision making (87 percent versus 78 percent).
- Better at managing finances (83 percent versus 73 percent).

Because male direct sellers were more interested than were female direct sellers in a full-time direct selling job, these differences require further investigation to untangle a possible relationship between gender and full- versus part-time direct selling job preferences; as such, they have implications for direct selling companies.

General Discussion

Direct sellers constitute a subset of gig workers and, analogous to gig workers, generally tend to be independent contractors pursuing part-time jobs. As such, direct sellers possess virtually the same demographic characteristics as do other gig workers. Moreover, direct sellers tend to share the same motivations as do other gig workers—the desire to earn "extra money" through a mechanism that offers work flexibility. This observation is perhaps the foremost "takeaway" from this chapter.

Direct sellers are not, as many in the popular press and on social media would have one believe, demons or people intent on taking unfair advantage of others through pyramid-like schemes (e.g., Tiffany 2020; Vesoulis and Dockterman 2020). Rather, they are, in most regards, merely a large (6.8 million) subset of gig workers driven by the same factors and motivations that drive gig workers generally. Additionally, like the gig economy and the gig workers that populate this economy, there exists heterogeneity among direct sellers. Even so, there are certain commonalities across direct sellers that merit consideration. Direct selling predates and helped form what we now know as the "gig economy." In that context, the channel should be considered a time-tested viable alternative in the context of the gig economy rather than an unrelated phenomenon.

What emerges from the gig survey and the reflections presented in this chapter is perhaps a somewhat nuanced picture of direct selling and direct sellers. The picture is termed "somewhat nuanced" because it is based on a relatively small number of direct sellers. As documented by the gig survey results presented in this chapter, direct sellers and other gig workers are relatively similar with respect to demographic characteristics, motives for entering the gig economy, gig income expectations and actual income, and satisfaction with their gig (as indicated by how they rated their gig experience and whether they would recommend their gig to others).

The direct seller survey results both complement and supplement the gig survey results (and both surveys support the inferences that can be drawn from the individual direct seller reflections). Most notably, the direct seller survey results demonstrate that a direct selling experience can enhance an individual's personal life self-efficacy and improve performance on nondirect selling jobs. At the same time, the results of the direct seller survey reveal differences in perceived benefits (improvements in self-efficacy) between male and female direct sellers.

Answers to the Questions

The chapter concludes with answers to the three rhetorical questions posed: (1) Why do people become direct sellers? (2) What do direct sellers expect to earn when they enter the gig economy, and what do they actually earn from their "direct selling gig?" and (3) Does a direct selling experience improve an individual's personal life self-efficacy?

Why do people become direct sellers? Answers to this question come from the gig survey and the direct seller survey. People become direct sellers to obtain financial and nonfinancial benefits. The financial benefits are earnings derived from direct selling activities. Because a substantial majority of direct sellers only work their direct selling gig part-time, typical goals include earning "extra money" that can be used to pay household bills, improve personal lifestyles, save or invest, or be allocated in numerous other ways. However, the desire for "extra money" is only one of the reasons people become direct sellers and, in point of fact, this desire does not always seem to be the most important reason. Several nonfinancial reasons also appear to be the drivers behind someone becoming a direct seller. Indeed, there is some evidence that, at least for a segment of direct sellers, nonfinancial reasons for becoming a direct seller dominate financial reasons for becoming a direct seller. These nonfinancial reasons include a desire to purchase products or services at a discount from a favored company, a desire to share the products or services of the favored company with others, and a desire for social affiliation.

What do direct sellers expect to earn when they enter the gig economy, and what do they actually earn from their "direct selling gig?" Answers to this question are derived from the gig survey. In general, direct sellers, like other gig workers, appear to be realistic regarding money to be earned from a direct selling gig. Nearly 71 percent of the direct sellers expected to earn less than US$500 per month from their gig, consistent with findings that direct selling tends to be a part-time supplemental earning opportunity, undertaken to obtain incremental money, and, for a plurality of direct sellers, accounts for less than 10 percent of their household income. Moreover, consistent with their expectations, about 73 percent of the direct sellers stated that they actually earned US$500 per month or less from their gig. More to the point, 80 percent of the direct sellers stated that they actually earned as much or more than they expected to earn when they entered the gig economy. This reality no doubt contributed to the finding that 93 percent of the direct sellers rated their direct selling experience as being a positive experience.

Does a direct selling experience improve an individual's personal life self-efficacy? Based on data from the direct seller survey, the answer appears to be "yes." A minimum of three-quarters of the direct sellers surveyed indicated that each of the 13 personal life skills studied benefitted from their direct selling experience. Additionally, of the direct sellers holding a nondirect selling job, 84 percent stated that their direct selling experience enhanced their performance on that job. Hence, given that the perceptions of personal life skills can be considered dimensions of self-efficacy, personal life self-efficacy was believed to have been improved through a direct selling experience.

Concluding Comments

Given the nonfinancial benefits that direct sellers seem to want when entering the gig economy, and appear to acquire as a consequence of their direct selling experience, it seems logical that a direct selling company should take this information into account when creating recruitment, training, and retention programs. For example, a direct selling company might emphasize (and communicate) the existence of nonfinancial benefits such as personal life skill improvements that can result from a direct selling experience as well as improved performance in nondirect selling jobs, regardless of direct selling success. While financial benefits are obviously part of any "package" used to recruit and reward direct sellers, a focus on nonfinancial benefits might be more productive for improving the performance of both direct sellers and their direct selling company.

References

Bandura, A. 1997. *Self-Efficacy: The Exercise of Control*. New York, NY: Freeman.

Benoit, S., T.L. Baker, R.N. Bolton, T. Gruber, and J. Kandampully. 2017. "A Triadic Framework for Collaborative Consumption (CC): Motives, Activities and Resources & Capabilities of Actors." *Journal of Business Research* 79, pp. 219–227.

Direct Selling Association. 2020. "DSA Growth & Outlook Report: U.S. Direct Selling in 2019," www.dsa.org/benefits/research (accessed November 1, 2020).

Duszynski, M. 2020. "Gig Economy: Definition, Statistics & Trends." https://zety.com/blog/gig-economy-statistics (accessed November 1, 2020).

Fleming, J.T. 2021. *Ultimate Gig: Flexibility, Freedom, Rewards*. Bingley, UK: Emerald Publishing.

Kuhn, K.M., and A. Maleki. 2017. "Micro-Entrepreneurs, Dependent Contractors, and Instaserfs: Understanding Online Labor Platform Workforces." *Academy of Management Perspectives* 31, no. 3, pp. 183–200.

Peterson, R.A. 2018. *Social Contributions of a Direct Selling Experience*. Washington, DC: Direct Selling Education Foundation.

Peterson, R.A. 2020. "Self-Efficacy and Personal Selling: Review and Examination with an Emphasis on Sales Performance." *Journal of Personal Selling and Sales Management* 40, no. 1, pp. 57–71.

Peterson, R.A., and T.R. Wotruba. 1996. "What is Direct Selling?—Definition, Perspectives, and Research Agenda." *Journal of Personal Selling & Sales Management* 16, no. 4, pp. 1–16.

Peterson, R.A., V.L. Crittenden, and G. Albaum. 2019. "On the Economic and Social Benefits of Direct Selling." *Business Horizons* 62, no.3, pp. 373–382.

Peterson, R.A., G. Albaum, and V.L. Crittenden. 2020. "Self-Efficacy Beliefs and Direct Selling Sales Performance." *International Journal of Applied Decision Sciences* 13, no. 4, pp. 448–463.

Tiffany, K. 2020. "This Will Change Your Life." *The Atlantic*, https://theatlantic.com/technology/archive/2020/10/why-multilevel-marketing-and-qanon-go-hand-hand/616885/ (accessed October 28, 2020).

Vesoulis, A., and E. Dockterman. 2020. "Pandemic Schemes." *Time*, pp. 85–91.

CHAPTER 7

Opportunities and Challenges in Direct Selling

Victoria L. Crittenden and William F. Crittenden

"Simply put, people have always 'sold' things to one another" (Day 2014, 60), and, as described in Chapter 2, direct selling has long been a means for individuals to build businesses through selling. Historically, direct selling companies have leveraged an independent salesforce, bypassing much of the traditional marketing-related costs (e.g., advertising) and averting the endless competitive battle for shelf space. However, as described in Chapters 3, 4, and 5, direct selling companies face tremendous opportunities and challenges, both of which are influenced by a variety of environmental forces and stakeholder interests. Direct selling organizations that have an employee and distributor culture ready to adapt to these externalities are positioned for future success.

According to Warford (2021), the direct selling channel demonstrates considerable flexibility to sustain income for entrepreneurs. To reflect systematically on the opportunities and challenges in maintaining this flexibility and entrepreneurial spirit, the approach adopted initially in this chapter follows the PESTEL analysis of macroenvironmental influences followed by a stakeholder impact analysis. Following this, four executives in the direct selling marketplace were engaged to discuss issues they see as opportunities and challenges.

Environmental Influences—PESTEL

Used by strategic management practitioners and scholars, PESTEL (Political, Economic, Social, Technological, Ecological, and Legal) analysis is a simple and effective tool to identify key external, macroenvironmental forces that affect an organization. As seen in Figure 7.1, these are the forces that create opportunities and challenges for a direct selling organization. These external forces will evolve and new issues will emerge over time. The framework allows direct selling managers to structure important issues and to consider the impact and probability of the occurrence of various externalities in the direct selling marketplace. Importantly, individual company managers can add company-specific issues to the framework. Although it is unlikely one could readily forecast Black Swan events, such as the COVID-19 pandemic, agile direct selling organizations enhance their ability to respond via an awareness supported by close relationships with suppliers, employees, independent distributors, customers, and regulators. Taleb (2012) would likely refer to direct selling companies that can take the challenges in the macroenvironment and benefit from them as opportunities as "antifragile" companies. It is important for direct selling companies to identify the external factors that will be influential to success and to exploit those factors opportunistically.

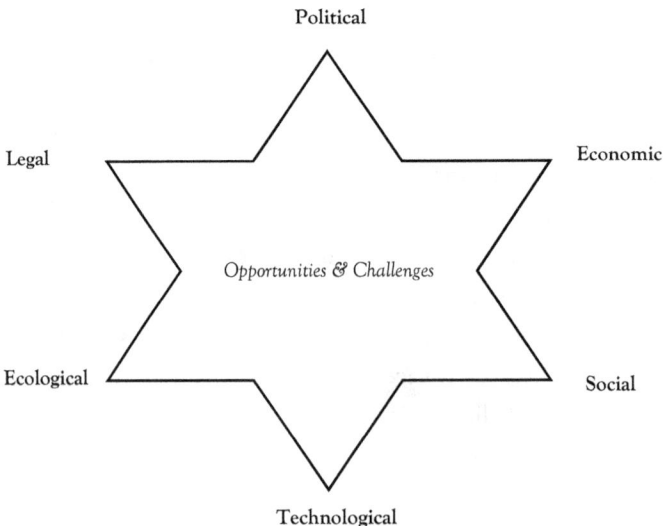

Figure 7.1 Macro-Environmental Forces—PESTEL

A sample PESTEL analysis for a direct selling company is offered in Table 7.1. This overall picture of the forces in the direct selling environment leads to several general outcomes. Although the direct selling marketplace continues to face new obstacles in this ever-evolving economy, the sector has an overall positive growth trend that will only be strengthened as it turns these challenges into opportunities for advancement.

From a *political* standpoint, there has been an increasing wariness of globalism around the world, as seen with the United Kingdom leaving the European Union (following Brexit), the ongoing trade wars between the United States and China, and the threat of other countries utilizing tariffs as a possible means of foreign policy. This global unease has the potential to inhibit direct selling companies from entering into new international markets. However, for companies already firmly in place across the globe, this should have a small impact since the direct selling marketplace tends to be highly resilient once it has taken root and adapted to the nuances of that international market. At the same time, the United States–Mexico–Canada Agreement (USMCA), which replaced the North American Free Trade Agreement (NAFTA), will likely have positive effects on trade and economic growth in North America.

The U.S. *economy* is doing reasonably well and growing steadily. Although this is favorable to the direct selling sector (and business in general), some warn that the economy is more fragile than it appears and that financial issues may lie ahead for all businesses. Nevertheless, consumer spending and retail sales have been continuing to grow in the United States, which greatly benefits direct selling companies. More specifically, there is evidence that direct selling is somewhat recession resistant since it has experienced growth in two of the three most recent recessions (Gamse 2020). Global expansion, as discussed in Chapter 5, has proven to be an important opportunity for many direct selling companies, with Asia/Pacific country markets, for example, providing approximately 44 percent of global direct selling revenue (World Federation of Direct Selling Associations 2020).

In terms of *social* demographics and values, many opportunities exist that facilitate the growth and advancement of direct selling companies. In particular, the rising popularity of the gig economy, as discussed in Chapter 6, and the growing entrepreneurial spirit all over the world,

Table 7.1 **PESTEL** *analysis*

	Specific itemized issues	Trend Ongoing/Stable	Impact Negative/Positive Low/Mod/High	Probability Low/Mod/High or 0–100%
Political	• Increasing wariness of globalism around the world (as seen with the U.S.–China trade war) decreases appeal of international markets	• Stable	• Moderate to low negative	• Moderate to high
	• U.S.–Mexico–Canada Agreement (USMCA) increases trade in North America	• Ongoing	• Moderate positive	• Moderate to high
	• New trade agreements to come between the UK and EU (following Brexit) will likely hurt the UK economy	• Ongoing	• Moderate to low negative	• Moderate to high
Economic	• U.S. economy steadily growing, which benefits businesses	• Stable	• Moderate to high positive	• Moderate
	• Consumer spending and retail sales continually increasing, which is favorable to direct selling	• Stable	• Moderate to high positive	• Moderate
Social	• Increasing popularity of the gig economy entrepreneurship can add greatly to the direct selling workforce	• Stable	• Moderate to high positive	• Moderate to high
	• More emphasis on products and employment that are enriched by social causes	• Ongoing	• Moderate positive	• Low to moderate
	• A focus on company culture	• Ongoing	• High	• Moderate to high

Technological	• Advanced technologies have led to the rise of e-commerce giants (e.g., Amazon, eBay)	• Ongoing	• Moderate to high negative	• High
	• Growing importance of science and research to create and improve upon high-quality products	• Ongoing	• Moderate to low negative	• Moderate
Ecological	• Growing concern about environmental impacts of business (chemical-use, waste, pollution, reusable/biodegradable, etc.)	• Ongoing	• Moderate to low negative	• Moderate
	• Consumers increasingly wanting all natural or organic ingredients in their products	• Ongoing	• Moderate to low negative	• Moderate
Legal	• Scrutiny with regards to worker classification and compensation	• Ongoing	• Moderate to high negative	• High
	• Increased scrutiny over compliance and accurate representation of product that could result in lawsuits	• Ongoing	• Moderate to high negative	• High
	• Higher regulatory standards for direct selling companies, especially in international markets, can hurt business	• Ongoing	• Moderate to high negative	• Moderate

as noted in Chapter 1, offers many new avenues for the direct selling salesforce. Additionally, there is more emphasis on social causes, where consumers want to buy ethical products and employees/independent distributors want to do meaningful work and be part of a community. This presents an opportunity for the direct selling companies to differentiate themselves and use the personal touch to attract both customers and distributors alike.

The advancement of *technologies* has clearly challenged the typical direct selling model, as seen with the rise of e-commerce giants such as Amazon and eBay. However, if direct selling companies continue to adapt and utilize technology in a way that complements their natural business strategies, these businesses can improve significantly. Opportunities for technology integration in direct selling include: e-commerce and online shopping to sell products, data analytics to improve product development and marketing, mobile-friendly apps and websites to improve communication with customers and distributors, virtual assistance programs to enhance customer service capabilities, social media branding to increase brand and product awareness, improved manufacturing processes, and distributor training simulations (to name a few). Additionally, technology is useful to enhance research and development of high-quality products to improve the capabilities of products to meet the needs of consumers. As suggested by Ferrell and Ferrell (2012), it is important to pair the right technological platform with the right stakeholder, as will be discussed in the next section.

Increasingly, people are more and more concerned about the *environment* and the health impact of products. Thus, direct selling companies are challenged to source more natural and organic ingredients, eliminate chemical and biohazardous waste, create innovative packaging that is reusable/biodegradable, and, in general, reduce their carbon footprint. While this will take time, research, and resources for companies to master, doing so can be a high value-add point of differentiation that attracts customers and distributors while also affecting the environment positively.

Lastly, as with all companies, the direct selling marketplace is closely impacted by the *legal* frameworks regulating how business should be conducted. In general, businesses are facing increased regulation from both the public and the government to ensure they are not violating compliance standards or misrepresenting their products. Any company that breaches these rules of conduct can face hefty fines and even civil suits. Furthermore, direct selling companies tend to face even higher levels of scrutiny from governments due to fears of pyramid schemes. Currently, as will be described in the stakeholder analysis, there is intense scrutiny regarding the gig economy and employee compensation, which directly affects direct selling companies. Direct seller's leadership in self-regulation can help avoid cumbersome constraints often imposed by government legal regulations.[1]

Stakeholder Impact Analysis

Knowing who the stakeholders are in the direct selling marketplace and understanding what these stakeholders expect from direct selling companies is critical to success, and direct selling companies are responsible to a wide variety of stakeholders (Freeman 1984). Stakeholder theory is grounded on the normative assumption that "all persons or groups with legitimate interests participating in an enterprise do so to obtain benefits and that there is no prima facie priority of one set of interests and benefits over another" (Mitchell, Agile, and Wood 1997, 68). An individual or group is considered a stakeholder when any one of the following three characteristics applies:

1. The actor has the potential to be positively or negatively affected by organizational activities and/or is concerned about the organization's impact on their or others' well-being;
2. The actor can withdraw or grant resources needed for organizational activities; and
3. The actor is valued by the organization (Frooman 1999).

Table 7.2 provides a stakeholder impact analysis for direct selling companies. Stakeholders identified for this analysis were: Management, Customers, Employees, Independent Distributors, Investors and Shareholders, Members of the Supply Chain, Government, and Societies and Communities. According to Crittenden, Crittenden, Ferrell, Ferrell, and

---

[1] Compensation, compliance, and ethics were discussed in greater detail in Chapters 3 and 4.

Table 7.2 Stakeholder impact analysis

Who are our stakeholders? (Material impact on us or us on them)	What economic, legal, ethical and philanthropic responsibilities do we have to our stakeholders?	What are their interests?	What opportunities and threats do our stakeholders represent?	What steps should we take to address our stakeholder's concerns?
Management	• Ensure that management is well compensated and equipped to handle leading the company and making major business decisions	• High financial compensation, respected status, and stability that comes from managing a successful company	• Management determines the long-term direction and strategy of the company so it's important that they're able to make shrewd and creative business decisions that lead to long-term growth and profitability	• Utilize technology and business analytics to better streamline management's responsibilities and also to help them understand the company's current performance, future trends, and problem solving • Better compensation plan for effective and higher-performing members of management
Customers	• Ensure that customers have a high-quality product that properly addresses their needs	• High-quality, effective products • Meaningful, convenient buying experience	• Opportunity to create a loyal base of customers that then go on to further promote the brand and possibly become independent distributors • Opportunity to have direct feedback from consumers on business functions so that the company can then improve in regard to product development, buying experience, marketing, and so on.	• Increased branding with a focus on providing information that is more valuable to customers (advice, product news and offerings, compelling story telling, answer questions, etc.) • Utilize technology and social media to create unique buying experiences (e-commerce, suggested products, mobile-friendly apps, easy to navigate websites, etc.) • Focus on more science and research to develop improved products that properly meet people's wellness and health need (de-stress, sleep, focus, etc.)

Employees	• Provide them with a good working environment along with pay and benefits	• Stable job • Livable wages and good benefits • Meaningful work	• Opportunity to create a highly skilled (long-term) workforce that's very passionate and knowledgeable about the company	• Keep them informed of business decisions (especially those regarding product development, branding, and selling strategies) • Provide good compensation and benefits
Independent distributors	• Have clear outlines of their responsibilities and compensation as sellers for the company	• Maintain independent contractor status • Flexible source of income • Feel like a fairly treated and valued part of the company workforce	• Increasing number of individuals with an entrepreneurial spirit and desire for flexible income sources that could be interested in becoming sellers • They are the primary point of contact between the business and the customers, which means the quality of their personalized service and product expertise are instrumental to branding and raising revenue	• Improve the recruitment and training process so that sellers feel well-prepared to represent the business • Enhance seller performance by revamping compensation/incentive programs and by looking into performance appraisal and retraining programs • Help them use their own technology and social media platforms to improve their selling performance
Investors and shareholders	• Important to keep them informed of the company's financial position and also want to give them the highest return on investment possible	• Essentially concerned with continued growth and profitability	• High concern with profitability might attract investors that buy and then sell quickly at the "peak," leaving companies searching for capital in the long term • In general, though there has been increased investment interest in DS companies so this presents a valuable opportunity to get more funding and more expertise	• Continued transparency of financial records and statements • Improving business and thus profits (e.g., better supply chain management, offshoring peripheral tasks to better focus on marketing and selling, utilizing technology, etc.) • Consider expansion into new markets (domestic or international) as a strategic way to gain revenue from previously untapped customers

(Continued)

Table 7.2 (*Continued*)

Members of the supply chain (raw ingredients, transportation, etc.)	• Have fair contracts with other businesses in the supply chain that lays out clear expectations of their responsibilities and our compensation in return	• Desire to have a stable partner that they can rely on to provide an avenue for business	• Smooth and effective supply chain management has the ability to reduce costs and improve the overall functioning of the business (no inventory shortages, on-time delivery, etc.)	• Utilize technology to better streamline/automate supply chain management • Consider outsourcing more peripheral business functions so that primary focus of company can be on marketing and selling the products
Government	• Be in compliance with any laws and regulations set forth by the government concerning how the business should be run	• Collect taxes from companies • Regulate businesses to make sure they're run in an ethical way and offer valid products • Protect consumer interests	• Direct selling companies often face higher levels of regulation (especially in international markets) due to a fear that they are/may become fraudulent pyramid schemes • Due to growing ecological concerns, governments may implement stricter environmental standards (regarding waste, pollution, etc.) • Particularly, the FDA will likely scrutinize more closely any cosmetic and wellness companies selling products that claim health benefits	• Management should have a clear understanding of all the laws that affect their business (taxes, environments, worker conditions, product quality, marketing claims, etc.) • Management also must make employees and distributors adequately aware of government regulations and train accordingly
Societies and communities (especially those within which independent distributors and/or consumers are based)	• Have a positive impact on the communities they interact with	• Well-developed businesses that provide products of value to consumers • Businesses that strengthen the community economically, socially, and environmentally	• Business and communities form a virtuous cycle, where firms can help improve the lives of their employees and customers and in turn stronger communities help businesses	• Companies should seek to empower more people through gainful work opportunities • Businesses also should consider giving back to communities through philanthropic measures and social programs

Pinney (2011), stakeholders are embedded directly or indirectly in inter-connected networks of relationships, with the diversity of concerns having to align for the well-being of the organization. Thus, actions that affect one direct selling stakeholder are likely to reverberate with other stakeholders.

As one example of the intertwining nature of stakeholders in the direct selling arena, the gig economy, as discussed in Chapter 6, has become an important topic of public interest and scrutiny. Noting that not all inde-pendent work is the same, protecting the independent worker status for all direct sellers is something for which the Direct Selling Association (DSA) has engaged considerably with the U.S. government. As described in previous chapters, the DSA is the national trade association for com-panies that market products and services directly to consumers through an independent sales force. In 2019, 125 people representing 19-member companies of the DSA met with members of the U.S. Congress to empha-size the importance of protecting independent workers. The following statement by Joseph Mariano, president and chief executive officer of the DSA, clearly depicts the interconnected network of stakeholders (DSN Staff 2019):

> Choice is a critical distinction to make, and H.R. 3522 preserves the direct sellers' ability to choose the products they want to sell, the customers they engage with, and the hours they will work—and make those decisions based on their own needs, responsibili-ties, and aspirations.

After the tumultuous year of 2020 with social distancing as the new normal, Luce (2020) had optics on the independent distributor stake-holder in relation to the company's (e.g., management's) ability to drive technology as a force for change. Loss of jobs meant more people at home, yet the desire for income and virtual selling opportunities set the stage for a safe, work-from-home opportunity to become an independent distributor. "Going virtual" meant the need to improve digital tools for everything from online training, online parties, and virtual conferences (Gamse 2020). While no one predicted the events of 2020 (e.g., pan-demic and social unrest), it is no surprise that Duncan (2019) had already acknowledged, "Overall, it's clear that direct selling is a digital marketing industry." With that came the focus on building, training, and utilizing advances in technology—a variable that affected numerous stakeholders.

As evidenced in Table 7.2, macroenvironmental factors within the PESTEL analysis have the potential to impact a variety of stakeholders in the direct selling community. The PESTEL and stakeholder analyses were conducted via an outsider-looking-in methodological approach utilizing secondary data. Now, we turn to an insider perspective on opportunities and challenges in the direct selling marketplace.

A View From the Top

According to a recent report by the Direct Selling Association (2020), "the global recession and drastic shifts in consumer behavior brought on by COVID-19 accelerated several existing trends and created both new challenges and new opportunities." To gain an insider perspective on opportunities and challenges in direct selling, in-depth, semistructured interviews were conducted with four key executives who have diverse experiences in the direct selling marketplace.

The interviewees included:

- *Angela Loehr Chrysler*, President and CEO, Team National— Team National is a membership savings company that utilizes the group buying power of its members (individuals, families, and businesses) to cut expenses and receive cash rebates.
- *Albert DiLeonardo*, CEO and President Vector East, Vector Marketing Corporation—Vector Marketing Corporation markets CUTCO Cutlery, a line of high-quality kitchen cutlery, accessories, and sporting knives.
- *Asma Ishaq*, CEO, Modere—Modere is a category-leading, global, live-clean essential lifestyle brand of supplements, household, and personal care products.
- *Gordon Hester*—global entrepreneur and business strategist with extensive field and corporate expertise in direct sales and network marketing.

According to these direct selling experts, three major forces comprise the opportunities and challenges in direct selling: social trends, technology, and the legal environment. The Direct Selling Association (2020) identified three key consumer trends driving direct selling growth (i.e., changing shopping behavior, focus on health, and interest in supplemental income) that fall into the social trends and technology challenges and opportunities areas identified by the four experts. Hester (2020, 122) referred to the "tragedy of the commons," where a few companies engaging in harmful practices have damaged the reputation of the direct selling marketplace as a whole. Thus, the legal (regulatory) environment was noted as a challenge that also presented an opportunity for direct selling companies.

Social—It's the People

Modere's business model relies on the opportunities afforded by social interactions, and Asma Ishaq said this is because "people make purchasing decisions based on their trust in other people." Building on this influenced-based marketing approach, Modere relies on the authenticity of its microinfluencers to lead with the company's products in their social marketing. Leading with strong, scientifically substantiated products ensures that the company's social marketers are building a foundation of trust within a highly segmented customer base where customer data are leveraged to create value for the customers, independent distributors, and company.

When asked what gets her excited about direct selling, Angela Chrysler (Team National) spoke about the social aspects of direct selling:

> What we get to do is relationship building that is culture driven. It is much more transformational than it is transactional. The transformational aspects of the variety of products and services that we have at our company, and the variety of products and services in direct selling as a whole, are very exciting. Added to that transformational relationship building, I love hearing about the beliefs that people have in themselves, the personal growth that they have in themselves and how we, as an industry, really help make people better people. We help them be their best version of themselves.

This trust in people is what Chrysler sees as the "truly endless" opportunity available in direct selling.

Al DiLeonardo (Vector Marketing) spoke about social issues, encapsulated as culture, when talking about the company's customers and the people within the company. In DiLeonardo's words, "the company culture is the soul of the company." As a direct seller, CUTCO/Vector had long held to the belief that customers needed to touch the product in the buying process and that sales training needed to be in person. Keeping abreast of societal changes, however, the company had begun investing heavily in a technological infrastructure. This investment paid off when the pandemic hit in 2020. The company was able to shift rapidly due to both sales training and product demonstrations being conducted virtually. These shifts resulted in significant recruiting increases, with male recruits increasing by 18 percent and female recruits increasing by 79 percent.

The importance of people came through loud and clear in discussions with these executives. From a stakeholder perspective, customers, employees, and distributors are the social and cultural backbone of direct selling companies, and the opportunities afforded when great people combine with great products create a strong economic space worldwide. Equally clear were the opportunities generated by the intertwining of people and technology—where high-touch embraces high-tech (Ferrell and Ferrell 2012) and the digitalization of the direct selling business model (Crittenden, Crittenden, and Crittenden 2019).

Technology—We Have the Tools

DiLeonardo was exuberant about the opportunities available with technology. "What is amazing about our business is how it has transformed because of technology. We have sales representatives who have never touched the product, selling to customers who have never touched the product. We have had a virtual interview, a virtual demo, and a virtual office, but our virtual operations never caught on until it had to in 2020. It was great that we had the programs that we were able to take off the shelf and expand them as needed. Technology has caused us not to have boundaries—our sales reps are selling to more customers and our Vector leadership team is more readily available in terms of jumping into meetings and attending virtual conferences across the USA, for example.

Basically, we can impact so many more people." Vector Marketing Corporation had the tools readily available and the quick pivot in 2020 to virtual is something that has changed the company forever.

The endless possibilities for building a community with technology is something for which Chrysler was also excited. To Chrysler, "direct selling companies have some of the best people and best products, with wonderful opportunities for supplemental income." While she sees technology as enabling direct selling companies to engage in online retailing, the difference to her is that direct selling can help her build a stronger sense of community within the Team National family. Chrysler provided examples of being able to be in different states all on the same day, helping to build a community via technological affordances.

With approximately 85 percent of its sales direct-to-consumer, Ishaq noted that technology as a sales platform has always been critical to Modere. Additionally, with the company's reliance on its product advocates (influencers), the company is heavily digitized. Looking ahead, changes in technology and technological opportunities will continue to be a driving force within Modere's business model.

While technology has long been an opportunity for growth in direct selling companies, it was never more evident than in 2020 when both internal and external technological platforms paved the way for continued success. However, technology has also brought challenges to direct selling companies. For Vector Marketing, leadership was giving thought on how to keep the Vector culture alive at a time when there were managers and sales reps who only knew Vector via Zoom and who had never visited the factory or met the leadership team face-to-face. In DiLeonardo's words: "Every company has a soul, and the soul of our company includes developing the skills of college students. How do you deliver the soul of the company through Zoom? How do we make sure our new people get the opportunity to experience the Vector culture and feel a part of the Vector family?"

Additionally, for the direct selling marketplace in general, technology has enabled community hate sites to thrive. Researchers have examined negative electronic word-of-mouth (eWOM) within the context of community and brand hate websites, social networking groups, and opposition blogs (Kucuk 2015), and the phenomenon of anticommunities is expanding quickly as is the number of consumers engaging in online hate behavior (Dessart, Veloutsou, and Morgan-Thomas 2020). Unfortunately, direct selling has not been immune to hate communities, with stories told online that are often misleading or incomplete.

Unfortunately, it is not only the haters who make technology a challenge for direct selling companies as it can also be the lovers of direct selling. As discussed next, the legal (regulatory) environment can pose a challenge for direct sellers in terms of technology use. Having an independent salesforce blurs the lines in terms of posts on personal social networking sites that run contrary to guidelines set for the direct selling marketplace.

Legal—Self-Regulation Protects the Business Model

Chapters 3 and 4 covered the topics of compensation, ethics, and compliance, all of which coalesced within the legal/regulatory environment among the direct selling executives interviewed. On the one hand, the legal/regulatory environment in which direct selling firms operate is challenging to navigate; on the other hand, regulations can help protect the direct selling business model and the companies that do engage in self-regulation. Chrysler and DiLeonardo both articulated this tension.

For Chrysler, "What keeps me up at night on any given day is the regulatory environment. The reason is not that I do not want to follow best practices nor is it that I do not agree with the recommendations made. There are two reasons that keep me up at night. One, the grayness of the regulatory environment—I want to do what is right, I want to lead that way, and I want my field to know what to do. But, the regulations are not always black and white and that makes it difficult to be a leader. Two, there is the nature of having an independent sales force. Every day, I put my trust in other individuals to not only make sales, but to make sales correctly and follow the regulatory standards. And, on any given day, I am not sure they are going to do that. I have to just put my faith in them and give them the right information and the right tools to make that happen."

For DiLeonardo, the three constant challenges in the regulatory environment for all direct selling companies are the independent contractor status, product claims, and income claims. With regard to independent contractor status, DiLeonardo said, "We see attempts to legislate companies like Uber where drivers have to become Uber employees and that could lead to independent contractor challenges in direct selling." In terms of product claims, direct selling companies have to be very careful about what is attributed to the product's capabilities (e.g., eliminating wrinkles, reducing health risks, etc.). This is true for all consumer goods companies, but direct selling companies are hit especially hard because of the inherent lack of control over independent contractors. Income claims are another challenge DiLeonardo identified in direct selling. Interestingly, this challenge brings together the social and technology factors that have provided so many opportunities for direct sellers.

DiLeonardo offered an example of social and technology leading to a regulatory challenge. "For example, we go on one of our reward trips and the sales rep posts on his or her personal social media something like—'Thank you, Vector, for making this great trip to Paris possible. I love our company!' Or, sometimes, sales reps even post pictures of their bonus checks on their own social media accounts. Really, they are just so happy and want to let their family and friends know they are doing well. Unfortunately, those personal posts can be viewed as income claims and perceived by regulators as the company trying to recruit others, even though it is on a personal social media page and not a corporate-controlled communication." Thus, the uncontrolled communications made possible by successful, independent salespeople and social media create regulatory challenges for the company.

While Ishaq said that it was hard to control independent contractors, she viewed the regulatory environment as a major opportunity for the direct sellers to protect the business model. In particular, membership in the DSA keeps ethical direct selling companies from being "lumped in" with companies that are not adhering to high standards (DiLeonardo referred to this as the rogue startups that give direct selling a bad name). The vetting process to become a member company of the DSA is rigorous, and Ishaq is pleased with the latest addition to the oversight offered by the DSA with the Direct Selling Self-Regulatory Council (DSSRC) that launched in January 2019 as a partnership between the DSA and the Council for Better Business Bureaus.[2]

Social, Technology, and Legal—What Happens When It All Comes Together?

To wrap up this chapter on the opportunities and challenges in direct selling, Gordon Hester, author of *Positioned Right—The Forces Shaping the Future of Direct Selling and Network Marketing* (Hester 2020), offered his perspective on the three challenges and opportunities identified by the company Presidents/CEOs. Hester, who has worked in direct selling for many years as an entrepreneur, in management positions, and as a consultant, summarized his thoughts on the three opportunities and challenges as, "I think our industry has an educational gap."

Looking at the social perspective from the views of the field and the customer, Hester says that distributors do not understand compliance, which makes it difficult for them to follow best practices. However, he says, "they are craving to understand compliance because they do not want to do anything that puts them or their company in jeopardy." Linking technology to compliance, Hester says that direct selling companies can help their distributors via an app that flags a social media post, for example, before it goes live if it is a compliance risk. The app would then depict the risk and what needs to be done to make the post compliant. In this way, the company would be educating the field on how to use social media appropriately instead of the company having to "clean things up after-the-fact."

In terms of the customer, Hester thinks direct selling has some catching up to do with respect to really understanding the customer journey. Additionally, he feels "there is a massive opportunity for the industry to redefine itself by paying attention to the customer retention game." To educate companies about customers, Hester thinks there is a greater need to understand the data to move the focus to the lifetime value of the customer.

---

[2] Details about the DSSRC appear in Chapter 4.

Direct selling, according to Hester, has always been heavy on intuition. While intuition is great, technology can enable the capturing of so much customer data that can validate (or invalidate) management's intuition. Firm technology has changed dramatically over the years, and Hester thinks that direct selling companies would benefit from a greater focus on the overall architecture of the firm's technology; that is, learning to put pieces together so that the middleware is driving the technology. He says, "It is really about aligning the right tech strategy and people and then having the courage to invest in technology to facilitate a digital transformation of the company. With technology today, it is learning to put the pieces together so they can work in unison. Ultimately, what technology is designed to do is to support the people so they can be more successful for the field, for the customer, and for the operations of the firm."

Navigating the Future

The four direct selling experts identified several current external issues providing opportunities and challenges for direct selling companies (i.e., social, technological, and legal). A direct selling company's leadership must stay abreast of the ever-evolving macroenvironmental and stakeholder factors that can positively or negatively impact future organizational success. Identifying trends in their infancy can provide new opportunities for product development, cost savings, market expansion, or business model revision. Understanding these externalities also allows direct selling leaders to develop strategic plans appropriate for the challenges they face, whether now or in the near future. Organizations like the DSA can aid firms by researching and providing data on broad PESTEL factors and stakeholder trends on a country-market basis.

The PESTEL and stakeholder frameworks presented in this chapter provide a methodology for direct selling managers to structure issues that create company opportunities and challenges. While material presented within the frameworks will help managers recognize and understand current issues facing direct sellers, it is important to recognize that these factors will evolve, resulting in the need to update the external analysis on a periodic basis. It is also essential for managers to design the analyses to integrate company specific factors. By paying attention to externalities,

leaders of direct selling companies can approach change positively, resulting in positioning that allows them to seize opportunities as they arise.

References

Crittenden, A.B., V.L. Crittenden, and W.F. Crittenden. 2019. "The Digitalization
Triumvirate: How Incumbents Survive." *Business Horizons* 62, pp. 259–266.

Crittenden, V.L., W.F. Crittenden, L.K. Ferrell, O.C. Ferrell, and C.C. Pinney.
2011. "Marketing Oriented Sustainability: A Conceptual Framework
and Propositions." *Journal of the Academy of Marketing Science* 39, no. 1,
pp. 71–85.

Day, T. 2014. "The Evolution of Direct Selling." *Direct Selling News*, January,
pp. 60–66.

Dessart, L., C. Veloutsou, and A. Morgan-Thomas. 2020. "Brand Negativity: A
Relational Perspective on Anti-Brand Community Participation." *European
Journal of Marketing*, 54, no. 7, pp. 1761–1786.

Direct Selling Association. 2020. "Direct Selling in the United States – 2021 and
Beyond," https://dsa.org (accessed February 10, 2021).

DSN Staff. 2019. "Direct Sellers Urge Lawmakers to Protect and Clarify
Independent Contractor Status." *Direct Selling News*, https://directsellingnews.
com/direct-sellers-urge-lawmakers-to-protect-and-clarify-independent-
contractor-status/ (accessed January 17, 2021).

Duncan, B. 2019. "The 10 Marketing Challenges Direct Sales Companies are
Taking On in 2020." https://worldofdirectselling.com/marketing-challenges-
direct-sales/ (accessed January 17, 2021).

Ferrell, L., and O.C. Ferrell. 2012. "Redirecting Direct Selling: High-Touch
embraces High-Tech." *Business Horizons* 55, no. 3, pp. 273–281.

Freeman, R.E. 1984. *Strategic Management: A Stakeholder Approach*. Boston:
Pitman.

Frooman, J. 1999. "Stakeholder Influence Strategies." *Academy of Management
Review* 24, no. 2, pp. 191–205.

Gamse, B. 2020. "The State of Direct Selling and Envisioning the Future of
the Channel." *Direct Selling News*, https://directsellingnews.com/the-state-of-
direct-selling-and-envisioning-the-future-of-the-channel/ (accessed January
17, 2021).

Hester, G.D. 2020. *Positioned Right – The Forces Shaping the Future of Direct
Selling and Network Marketing*. Sarasota, FL: Hester Consulting Services,
LLC.

Kucuk, S.U. 2015. "A Semiotic Analysis of Consumer-Generated Antibranding."
Marketing Theory 15, no. 2, pp. 243–264.

Luce, W.A. 2020. "2021: A Year of Chance, Change, & Challenges." *Direct Selling News*, https://directsellingnews.com/2021-a-year-of-chance-change-challenges/ (accessed January 17, 2021).

Mitchell, R.K., B.R. Agle, and D.J. Wood. 1997. "Toward a Theory of Stakeholder Identification and Salience: Defining the Principle of Who and What Really Counts." *Academy of Management Review* 22, no. 4, pp. 853–886.

Taleb, N.N. 2012. *Antifragile: Things that Gain from Disorder*. London: Penguin.

Warford, J.L. 2021. "Continuing the Momentum of Pandemic Growth." *Social Selling News*, https://socialsellingnews.com/link/continuing-the-momentum-of-pandemic-growth-2639/ (accessed January 13, 2021).

World Federation of Direct Selling Associations. 2020. "Global Direct Selling—2019 Retail Sales." https://wfdsa.org/wp-content/uploads/2020/07/Sales-Seller-2020-Report-Final.pdf (accessed January 17, 2021).

About the Authors

Sara L. Cochran is a Clinical Assistant Professor in the Department of Management and Entrepreneurship in the Kelley School of Business at Indiana University and serves on the Board of Directors of the United States Association for Small Business and Entrepreneurship (USASBE). Sara is a Fellow with the Direct Selling Education Foundation and represents the Kelley School in the Indiana Startup Ladies. In addition to serving as a Contributing Editor for the *Journal of Entrepreneurship Education and Pedagogy (EE&P)*, Sara's research has been published in the *Journal of Small Business Management, Annals of Entrepreneurship Education and Pedagogy, EE&P, Entrepreneur & Innovation Exchange*, and *Go-to-Market Strategies for Women Entrepreneurs*. In the Kelley School, Sara is an affiliated faculty member of the Johnson Center for Entrepreneurship and Innovation, advises the IU chapter of the Collegiate Entrepreneurs Organization, and serves on the undergraduate policy committee. Sara has been awarded the Association for Research in Business Education Dissertation Award, the Emerging Scholar Award from the USASBE Minority and Women Entrepreneurship Special Interest Group, a Schulze Publication Award, a DSEF Best Paper Award, and was a 2019 *Columbia Business Times*'s 20 Under 40 Honoree. An entrepreneur herself, Sara founded and previously owned an online boutique and currently operates a consulting brand. She holds a PhD in entrepreneurship education from the University of Missouri, as well as a BA in accounting and an MA in integrated marketing communications from Drury University.

Anne T. Coughlan is the Polk Bros. Chair in Retailing and Professor of Marketing, Emerita at the Kellogg School of Management. Dr. Coughlan's main research interests are in the areas of distribution channels, sales force management and compensation, and pricing. Her coauthored work on "Direct Selling Distributors: Why Do They Stay or Leave?" won the best doctoral-student paper award at the 2017 Global Sales Science Institute conference. Dr. Coughlan is a coauthor of the book, *A Field Guide to Channel Strategy: Building Routes to Market* (with Sandy Jap), and was the lead author of *Marketing Channels* (a Prentice-Hall textbook) through its seventh edition. She serves on the Senior Advisory Board of the *Journal of Personal Selling & Sales Management* and is Editor-in-Chief of the SSRN Marketing Research Network and of its Quantitative Marketing e-Journal and the Marketing Science e-Journal. She is a Research Fellow of the Direct Selling Education Foundation and an Institute of Marketing Research Fellow of the University of Muenster, Germany. She has served as an Associate Editor and editorial board member of *Marketing Science* and on the editorial boards of *Journal of Marketing* and *Journal of Retailing*. For her excellence in teaching, Dr. Coughlan was the recipient of the school's Executive Master's Program Teacher of the Year Award for the best elective course in 1996 and again in 2003, as well as receiving the Sidney J. Levy Teaching Award in 2000–2001.

Victoria (Vicky) Crittenden is Professor of Marketing and Babson Research Scholar at Babson College. Vicky's research appears extensively in journals such as the *Journal of the Academy of Marketing Science, Marketing Letters, Sloan Management Review, Psychology & Marketing, Business Horizons, Entrepreneurship Theory & Practice, Journal of Business Research,* and *Journal of Personal Selling & Sales Management*. Her educational scholarship appears in such journals as the *Journal of Marketing Education, Marketing Education Review, Decision Sciences Journal of Innovative Education, Journal of Education for Business, Journal of Teaching in International Business,* and *Journal for Advancement of Marketing Education*. Vicky is editor of *Go-to-Market Strategies for Women Entrepreneurs: Creating and Exploring Success* published by Emerald Group Publishing in 2019. Additionally, she currently serves as Editor of the *Journal of Marketing Education*. Vicky was honored to receive the AMS CUTCO/ Vector Distinguished Marketing Educator Award in 2021, AMA Higher Ed SIG Lifetime Achievement Award in 2021, Circle of Honor award from the Direct Selling Education Foundation in 2019, AMA's Pearson Prentice Hall's Solomon-Marshall-Stuart Award for Innovative Excellence in Marketing Education in 2013, AMS Distinguished Fellow in 2008,

AMS Lamb, Hair, McDaniel Outstanding Marketing Teacher Award in 2005, and Lyon College Distinguished Alumna Award in 1999. Vicky is a member of the Academic Advisory Board for CUTCO/Vector Marketing Corporation and serves on the Board of Directors of the Direct Selling Education Foundation. She previously served on the Harvard Business School Alumni Board, the Board of Trustees at Lyon College, and the Faculty Advisory Board for Emerald Group Publishing. She is a past president of the Academy of Marketing Science and past Chair of the AMA Teaching & Learning Special Interest Group.

An advisor to various private, public, and nonprofit organizations, **William F. Crittenden** has worked with organizations such as BAE Systems, Boston Beer Company, Boston Management Consortium, Lotus Software (IBM), Head Start, and Wal-Mart Stores. He also has worked with Funducion CANE in Buenos Aires, Argentina and Banco Nacional de Comercio Exterior of Monterrey, Mexico. Bill has served in various university administrative posts, including Senior Associate Dean and Dean of Faculty and Dean for Graduate Business Programs at Northeastern University where he is a Professor of International Business and Strategy. He currently serves on the advisory board of Orphans Futures Alliance (a 501 (c) 3). He has served on the advisory board of a software start-up and as a trustee on a charitable, fraternal nonprofit organization. Bill is a member of numerous professional organizations including the Strategic Management Society (founding member) and the Academy of Management. He is a former Chair of the Public & Nonprofit Division of the Academy of Management. He has served in a variety of associate editor, guest editor, and reviewer roles and currently serves on the Editorial Review Board for *Business Horizons* and is on the Advisory Board for *Nonprofit Management & Leadership.* He has authored or coauthored over 60 journal publications, a strategic planning workbook, and numerous book chapters/sections and business cases. His articles have appeared in academic outlets including *Strategic Management Journal, Entrepreneurship Theory & Practice, Journal of Business Ethics,* and *Journal of the Academy of Marketing Science* and practitioner outlets such as *Business Horizons, Industrial Management,* and *Journal of Personal Selling & Sales*

Management. Bill was voted one of *Favorite Professors at Northeastern* by the Senior Class of 2014, Cauldron Yearbook, and he was the winner of the *Beta Gamma Sigma Teacher of the Year* in 2002.

Linda K. Ferrell is the Roth Family Professor of Marketing and Business Ethics at Auburn University. She served on the faculty at Belmont University, University of New Mexico, University of Wyoming, University of Northern Colorado, Colorado State University, and University of Tampa. She comanaged two $1.25 million grant for business ethics education through the Daniels Fund Ethics Initiative at the University of New Mexico with her husband, O.C. Ferrell. She was also jointly responsible for securing over $5 million for the first Bill Daniels Distinguished Professor Chair of Business Ethics at the University of Wyoming. Her research interests include marketing ethics, ethics training and effectiveness, the legalization of business ethics as well as corporate social responsibility and sustainability. She has published in the *Journal of the Academy of Marketing Science, AMS Review, Journal of Business Ethics, Journal of Public Policy & Marketing, Journal of Business Research,* as well as others. She has coauthored numerous books including *Business Ethics: Ethical Decision Making and Cases* (12th edition), *Business and Society* (4th edition), *and Introduction to Business* (12th edition). Professionally, Ferrell served as an account executive in advertising with McDonald's and Pizza Hut's advertising agencies in Houston, Indianapolis, and Philadelphia. She was recently honored as the Innovative Marketer of the Year for the Marketing Management Association. Ferrell has served on the Board of Directors of Mannatech, Inc., a NASDAQ-listed health and wellness company. She serves on the Board of the National Association of State Boards of Accountancy-Center for the Public Trust. She serves on the Executive Committee, Board, and Academic Advisory Committee of the Direct Selling Education Foundation. She is on the CUTCO/Vector Academic Advisory Board. She is past president of the Academy of Marketing Science and past president of the Marketing Management Association. Ferrell also serves as an expert witness in ethics and legal disputes.

O.C. Ferrell is the James T. Pursell, Sr. Eminent Scholar in Ethics and Director of the Center for Ethical Organizational Cultures at Auburn University. He has served on the faculty at Belmont University, the University of New Mexico, University of Wyoming, Colorado State University, University of Memphis, Texas A&M University, University of Michigan, Illinois State University, and Southern Illinois University. O.C. is immediate past president of the Academy of Marketing Science. He was formerly vice president of publications for the Academy of Marketing Science and was past president of the Academic Council of the American Marketing Association. He serves on the board of the National Association of State Boards of Accountancy's Center for the Public Trust and is an advisory board member of Savant Learning. Additionally, he serves on the Academic Advisory Committee for the Direct Selling Education Foundation. He received the AMS CUTCO/Vector Distinguished Educator Award for contributions to the marketing discipline. Additional recognition includes being the first recipient of the Marketing Education Innovation Award for the Marketing Management Association, Lifetime Achievement Award from the Macromarketing Society, and special award for service to doctoral students from the Southeast Doctoral Consortium. O.C. is coauthor of several leading textbooks including *Business Ethics: Ethical Decision Making and Cases* (12th edition), *Marketing* (19th edition), *Marketing Strategy* (6th edition), *Business and Society* (4th edition), *Management* (3rd edition), and *Introduction to Business* (12th edition). He has published in the *Journal of Marketing, Journal of Marketing Research, Journal of the Academy of Marketing Science, Journal of Business Ethics, Journal of Public Policy & Marketing, AMS Review, Journal of Business Research,* as well as others. He writes weekly business ethics summaries and reviews for the *Wall Street Journal* with a subscriber list of over 6,000. O.C. has served as an expert witness in some high-profile ethics, legal, and marketing cases.

W. Alan Luce is Senior Managing Principal of Strategic Choice Partners, LLC, (formerly Luce, Murphy Fong & Associates, LLC) a consulting firm dedicated to providing services to direct sellers and specializing in guidance for established and start-up organizations alike. As such, he has provided compensation plan design, sales force management, and strategic advice to more than 40 start-up, and dozens of existing, direct selling companies including Avon, Princess House, PartyLite Gifts, Inc., and Jockey Person 2 Person. In addition to his consulting practice, Luce has served on the Board of Directors of SimplyFun, LLC, Creative Memories, and Alcas Corporation (CUTCO/Vector), and on many direct selling company advisory boards. During his career, Mr. Luce has served as Senior Vice President of Sales & Marketing for PartyLite Gifts, Inc. and as the Founder and CEO of DK Family Learning, which he took from start-up to more than $30 million in sales in four years in the United States and over $80 million in sales worldwide. Prior to that Luce served at Tupperware Home Parties where he spent 16 years, rising to the position of Vice President of Administration and General Counsel. He began his career in direct selling as Associate General Counsel for the Direct Selling Association. In addition to his work with direct selling companies, Mr. Luce has long been active in the DSA and the Direct Selling Education Foundation, having served on the boards and as Chairman of both organizations. In 2002, he was recognized for his vision and leadership in DSEF when he was selected to receive the Circle of Honor award and during the 2005 DSA Annual Meeting, based upon his career of industry leadership and service, he was inducted into the Direct Selling Hall of Fame. He is a frequent industry spokesperson and expert lecturer at college and university business schools on behalf of the Direct Selling Education Foundation.

Robert A. Peterson holds the John T. Stuart III Centennial Chair at The University of Texas at Austin. He has served as Chairman of the Marketing Department, Associate Dean for Research, and Associate Vice President for Research and Research Integrity Officer, all at The University of Texas at Austin. He has published more than 200 books and peer-reviewed journal articles relating to marketing strategy and management, consumer behavior, and marketing research. Professor Peterson has served as editor-in-chief of two major academic marketing journals, the *Journal of Marketing Research* and the *Journal of the Academy of Marketing Science*, and as founding co-editor of a third academic marketing journal, the *AMS Review*. A Fellow of the American Marketing Association, he has received numerous awards for his research, including the Jagdish N. Sheth Award, the John D. C. Little Award, the McCombs School of Business Career Award for Outstanding Research Contributions, and the Portuguese Medal of Science. In 2019, a supercomputer was named for him ("BOB"). He has served as an officer in various professional academic associations, including service as president of the Academy of Marketing Science and as a member of an advisory committee to the United States Census Bureau. Dr. Peterson is a past member of the Direct Selling Education Foundation Board of Directors and was the first academic to be named to the Direct Selling Education Foundation Circle of Honor. An entrepreneur and active consultant, he presently owns or is a partner in several small businesses.

Index

OTHER TITLES IN THE SELLING
AND SALES FORCE MANAGEMENT COLLECTION

Naresh Malhotra, Georgia Tech, Editor

- *Rain Maker Pro* by Clifton Warren
- *How to be a Better Deal-Closer* by Simon P. Haigh
- *Entrepreneurial Selling* by Vincent Onyemah and Martha Rivera Pesquera
- *Selling: The New Norm* by Drew Stevens
- *How to Make Good Business Decisions* by Massimo Parravicini
- *Key Account Management* by Joel Le Bon and Carl Herman
- *Creating Effective Sales and Marketing Relationships* by Kenneth Le Meunier-FitzHugh and Leslie Caroline Le Meunier-FitzHugh
- *Improving Sales and Marketing Collaboration* by Avinash Malshe and Wim Biemans
- *Lean Applications in Sales* by Jaideep Motwani and Rob Ptacek
- *Competitive Intelligence and the Sales Force* by Joel Le Bon

Concise and Applied Business Books

The Collection listed above is one of 30 business subject collections that Business Expert Press has grown to make BEP a premiere publisher of print and digital books. Our concise and applied books are for...

- Professionals and Practitioners
- Faculty who adopt our books for courses
- Librarians who know that BEP's Digital Libraries are a unique way to offer students ebooks to download, not restricted with any digital rights management
- Executive Training Course Leaders
- Business Seminar Organizers

Business Expert Press books are for anyone who needs to dig deeper on business ideas, goals, and solutions to everyday problems. Whether one print book, one ebook, or buying a digital library of 110 ebooks, we remain the affordable and smart way to be business smart. For more information, please visit www.businessexpertpress.com, or contact sales@businessexpertpress.com.